CROSS MY HEART

A LITTLE WALK WITH JESUS

A COMPILATION OF ARTICLES AND DEVOTIONS

Melinda Eye Cooper

NEW HARBOR PRESS

RAPID CITY, SD

Copyright © 2023 Melinda Eye Cooper

All rights reserved. No part of this publication may be reproduced, distributed or transmitted in any form or by any means, including photocopying, recording, or other electronic or mechanical methods, without the prior written permission of the publisher, except in the case of brief quotations embodied in critical reviews and certain other noncommercial uses permitted by copyright law. For permission requests, write to the publisher, addressed "Attention: Permissions Coordinator," at the address below.

Cooper/New HarborPress
1601 Mt. Rushmore Rd, Ste 3288
Rapid City, SD 57701
www.newharborpress.com

Ordering Information:
Quantity sales. Special discounts are available on quantity purchases by corporations, associations, and others. For details, contact the "Special Sales Department" at the address above.

Cross My Heart/Melinda Eye Cooper. -- 1st ed.
ISBN 978-1-63357-283-6

Contents

Introduction 1

Five Truths a Man's Boots Reveal about His Heart 3

I've Fallen and I Can't Get Up 9

Five Heart Lessons from the Woman at the Well 15

Five Life Lessons I Wish I'd Learned before Fifty 23

Seven Marvelous Reasons to Celebrate Having a King 31

Seven Prayers for Christmas Dinner to Renew the
Hearts of Everyone Present 37

How Would Jesus Respond to Beggars? 45

Books of the Bible Every Senior Should Study 51

A Comforting Prayer for Miscarriages 59

Four Ways Jesus Calms the Storms in Our Lives 67

How to See What God Sees in You in a Culture of
Filters and Facebook Highlights 73

Three Lessons We Can Learn from Moses' Wife Zipporah 81

Four Lessons We Can Learn from Paul and Silas in Prison 89

Is It Biblical to Pray for Our Pets? 97

Is It Possible to Give Too Much? 105

Three Lessons We Can Learn from Noah's Drunkenness 111

How to Keep Your Sanity When Caring for a Loved
One with Alzheimer's 117

Five Truths We Can Take Away from King Solomon's Story 123

How to Let Go of Family Traditions and Embrace New Ones 131

How Do I Explain to Seekers Why My Church Asks for Money? ... 137

Three Ways We Can Guard Our Hearts 143

Six Reasons to Trust the Clay of Your Troubles in
the Potter's Hands 151

To Err Is Human 157

Can Anyone Really Be above Reproach? 163

Do Christians Care More about Looking Good
than Being Good? 169

What Is the Significance of Mount Moriah in the Bible? 175

How to Start a Prayer 183

How to Explain What the Holy Spirit Is 191

White Trash 197

I Got You 201

Middle-Aged Mama Moment 203

The Gift of a Boy 207

Lit 211

Seeds 215

Six Feet Apart 219

The Pressure Cooker 223

If the Good Lord's Willing 227

He Will Carry Me 231

The Heart of It 235

Super Salad!	237
If They Die	239
A Gift to Remember	243

Introduction

SHOULD I WRITE?

Sometimes, I get messages on my website asking how to become a writer. They want to know how they can get started. I love that they ask because it tells me something is nudging them to write and it may be God.

He spoke the world into existence with powerful words. His words accomplish incredible things. So, it's not far-fetched to think He may call us to write some powerful words, too.

> *As the rain and the snow come down from heaven, and do not return to it without watering the earth and making it bud and flourish, so that it yields seed for the sower and bread for the eater, so is my word that goes out from my mouth: It will not return to me empty, but will accomplish what I desire and achieve the purpose for which I sent it.* (Isaiah 55:10–11)

God indwells His children and may call us to write. With Him, our words will have power. Because He's guiding us and working through us. If we feel called to write, then we should surrender to it. Then get busy.

There are many online classes available. There are Christian writers' conferences to attend and writers' groups to join. There are free ways to begin writing a blog. We can share it on social media, receive feedback and learn. There will be negative comments and messages because people will always disagree about religion (and politics). Try to keep in the middle of the road and stick to biblical truth.

Once we've learned, then we submit our writing to something bigger than our personal blog. There are many places (especially online) to submit writing to begin accumulating writing credits for your writing resume. Plus, we're sharing our Christian experience with others and that's worth a million bucks all by itself without the writing credits.

This is a book filled with online work I've done. Mostly articles. But there are some devotions and a short Christmas story. I hope you enjoy it and I pray your spiritual journey is enhanced by reading the words God gave me to share.

> *Write down for the coming generation what the Lord has done, so that people not yet born will praise him. Psalms 102:18 (GNT)*

• CHAPTER 1 •

Five Truths a Man's Boots Reveal about His Heart

A sure sign of a hardworking man is a pair of worn, leather work boots. As with many folks, blue-collar roots run deep in our family. Dad spent many days and nights underground operating a drill in the lead mines. On weekends, he was a part-time pastor. His worn leather boots were by the door when he wasn't working or outside tending his garden.

My husband's steel-toed work boots were also found by the door nearly every night after driving a roll-off truck all day. Now, my middle son leaves his boots by the door, too. He makes his living as a welder.

I've seen a lot of pairs of leather boots sitting by the door over the years. And I love the hardworking men in my family. But what do all of those boots say about them?

Here are five truths a man's boots may reveal about his heart.

1. He's humble.

He may not love his job or even like it that much but he's not too proud to do some good old-fashioned hard work. He thinks of others before himself and that's why he works so hard.

He's willing to do what God asks him to do and is thankful for everything God has given him.

Humble yourselves before the Lord, and he will lift you up. (James 4:10)

2. He's genuine.

A good man wearing worn, leather work boots is *real*. He doesn't pretend to be something he's not. He believes it's always best to be truthful and kind.

He's does the best job he can do with the day God has given him and knows he's earned an honest living.

My steps have held to your paths; my feet have not stumbled. (Psalm 17:5)

3. He works hard.

He doesn't mind getting grease under his fingernails or dirt on his hands. He sure doesn't mind a farmer's tan. He gets up at the crack of dawn or even when it's still dark outside. He's willing to do whatever it takes to get the job done.

At night, he hits the sack exhausted. He's done his work with excellence and knows he represented God well with the work of his hands.

All hard work brings a profit, but mere talk leads only to poverty. (Proverbs 14:23)

4. He's a good provider.

He works overtime as often as he can get it. Some might think it's easy to do manual labor but physical work is *hard*. It can take a toll on a body.

He deals with body aches and strained muscles because he knows he's providing well for his family. A few back pains are worth it.

Give careful thought to the paths for your feet and be steadfast in all your ways. (Proverbs 4:26)

5. He loves his family.

A hardworking man loves his family. It's them he's thinking of when the alarm goes off and he forces himself out of bed on cold, winter mornings.

He thinks of them when he's working overtime and driving home after a long day on the job. His heart is full of love when he sees his children. He's thankful for his wife. Even though things aren't always perfect, he knows he is *blessed*.

He's a good dad and loves his family.

You will eat the fruit of your labor; blessings and prosperity will be yours. Your wife will be like a fruitful vine within your house; your children will be like olive shoots around your table. Yes, this will be the blessing for the man who fears the LORD. (Psalm 128:2–4)

BONUS Truth: He's a SERVANT at heart.

Jesus gave the greatest example of how to have a servant's heart by washing the feet of His disciples. In John 13:1–17, we read how Jesus went about it. It's interesting that Peter found it difficult to allow Jesus to wash his dirty feet. But when Jesus explained, he asked Jesus to not only wash his feet but to wash his hands and head as well.

A lot like Peter, it seems that sometimes hardworking men find it difficult to allow others to do anything for them. But his heart is in the right place.

The hardworking man demonstrates the heart of a servant.

- He serves God by seeking His will first in everything.
- He serves his wife by loving her and building a life together.
- He serves his children by providing for them and loving them.
- He serves his boss and coworkers by working hard each day.
- He serves his fellow man by doing hard work—whatever that may be.

He may spend his life working hard. He may spend it wearing worn, leather work boots. But whether he wears boots to work or not, he's a man with a strong desire to be like Jesus and to serve others.

Life goes by fast. Before he knows it, his children are grown with families of their own. He's not only a father but also a grandfather.

He'll enter a different stage of life and get to enjoy the fruits of his many years of labor.

When he retires, he'll still wear those old boots. Not because he needs them for work but because they've been a big part of his life. He finds a bit of himself in his worn leather work boots.

When he grows old and his mind is frail with age, he will still want to wear those old, worn-out boots. Or maybe he'll just wear one boot and a tennis shoe.

But the fact that he is still wearing the boot is a sure sign that he was a hardworking man, a good provider and a ***very good father.***

"His master replied, 'Well done, good and faithful servant! You have been faithful with a few things; I will put you in charge of many things. Come and share your master's happiness!' (Matthew 25:21)

MELINDA EYE COOPER

***This article was first published 9/24/2019 on Crosswalk.com

• CHAPTER 2 •

I've Fallen and I Can't Get Up

HAVE YOU EVER FALLEN *in public?*

I have. The year was 2014. I worked downtown in Nashville, Tennessee. My office building didn't provide parking, so each day I walked to and from the garage on 3rd Avenue.

I'm definitely not a city girl but I got so comfortable walking around downtown on a daily basis that it became routine.

One evening, after a tiring workday, I was almost at the garage entrance three blocks from my office when for no apparent reason—I fell.

There was nothing on the sidewalk in front of me that day to trip me up. I didn't stumble over anything. It was just me *forgetting* how to walk after many, many years of walking just fine.

Everything went into slow motion as I pitched forward with no control.

What's happening right now? Why am I falling in the heart of Music City with people everywhere? How can I stop this? Why did I wear a skirt today?

Then *splat*.

I wasn't yet to the place I needed to be, safe from public embarrassment.

I pelted the sidewalk with both knees and an elbow hitting first. My purse flew from my shoulder on impact and landed near me as I collapsed onto the sidewalk.

Dazed from the fall, I wiped my dirty hands on my skirt, picked up my purse, and got up as gracefully as possible. Then I dashed through the garage door without looking back.

Now, many years later, I look back on the whole embarrassing incident and believe I fell just short of the garage door for a *reason*. I was almost to the place I needed to be . . . but not quite.

God gave me a clear picture of my walk with Him. I fall short of His high standard. I'm far from perfect and sometimes quite clumsy.

If you, too, stumble in this life, here are four truths to hold onto for inspiration.

1. Even when you fall, God has you in the palm of His hand.

Every one of us will stumble at times in our Christian walk.

You may find yourselves reverting to old bad habits. Or even falling back into addiction after putting it behind you multiple times. We deal with our flesh daily. But God has given us the gift of the Holy Spirit to help us when we struggle.

And hope does not put us to shame, because God's love has been poured out into our hearts through the Holy Spirit, who has been given to us. (Romans 5:5)

2. We all fall short.

Any one of us can easily get tripped up in life. We may focus too much on the wrong things and not enough on God things. We give too much attention to what's going on around us instead of watching our own steps in our Christian walk.

For all have sinned and fall short of the glory of God. (Romans 3:23)

We all fall short of the glory of God because of the fallen state of the human race. Simply put—we're sinners. None of us are even close to perfect. But God's plan is perfect. I'm so thankful He provided a way *for us* through His Son.

None of us will ever walk so perfectly, without any tripping up whatsoever, as to be without sin. But every day, you have a mighty power working on your behalf to help you get back into step with your best life.

3. Jesus makes up for the shortfall.

Jesus lived up to God's high standard. He didn't sin and lived a perfect life we're incapable of living. He took our place on the cross and the punishment for all of our sin. He has your back by the stripes on His.

> *For God so loved the world that he gave his one and only Son, that whoever believes in him shall not perish but have eternal life. (John 3:16)*

- If we believe in Him, we'll trust Him.
- If we trust Him, we'll get to know Him.
- If we *know* Him, we will *love* Him.

The relationship that develops when we're in love with Jesus is the most amazing, precious gift. It's so much more than a simple blessing. It's more than anything we could ever hope for in this life. It's **everything**. God knows you're going to fall. He uses those moments to make you aware of His great love for you.

4. As believers, we walk by faith.

Truth is, you can envision, plan, and step boldly, but some of the best lessons in life are the ones that sidetrack or even throw you off your intended path. You won't always see in the moment how a fall can be redeemed. But, with your trust placed completely in Jesus Christ, you can stride the bumpy road of life with complete confidence. He is with you even when you fall. He will not leave you or forsake you. What a wonderful gift God has given! With prayer and patience, you grow closer to His walk for you. And even if you accrue some bruises and scars along the path, God will certainly bring beauty from your pain.

The Lord himself goes before you and will be with you; He will never leave you nor forsake you. Do not be afraid; do not be discouraged. (Deuteronomy 31:8)

When you find yourselves falling short of where you think you "should be by now" in your Christian walk, it's okay. Get up. Dust yourself off. Remember He is with you and makes up for any shortfall.

***This article was first published 11/4/2019 on Crosswalk.com

• CHAPTER 3 •

Five Heart Lessons from the Woman at the Well

AT TIMES, WE MAY need to have a heart-to-heart with someone we love.

Those conversations can be difficult. We may be afraid to say what's *needed* because we don't know how the other person might react when we get the courage to speak up. Maybe we don't want to hurt their feelings, but we can't continue without change in some way.

The longest one-on-one conversation Jesus had with someone in the Bible was with a *woman*. She went to the well to draw water and Jesus was waiting there.

Like many of us, she didn't know him very well. She'd heard of the Messiah but didn't realize He was right there with her. Her daily duties were keeping her occupied and He appeared in her life out of left field. She wasn't expecting Him to show up and she sure didn't expect Him to change her life.

But He was expecting her. He had plans she knew nothing about. He used her powerfully even though her life was far from picturesque.

It's an encouraging story and *beautiful*.

Encouraging to us because God allows us to participate in His work here on earth. It doesn't matter where we've been or what we've done in the past. He can use us and will for His purposes.

It's beautiful because when we have a *personal* relationship with Him, He gives us what we deeply need—the satisfying, living water to quench our spiritual thirst.

Here are five *heart* lessons we can learn from the woman at the well in the Bible.

1. We might find Jesus waiting for us.

> *Now he had to go through Samaria. So he came to a town in Samaria called Sychar, near the plot of ground Jacob had given to his son Joseph. Jacob's well was there, and Jesus, tired as he was from the journey, sat down by the well. It was about noon. When a Samaritan woman came to draw water, Jesus said to her, "Will you give me a drink?" (John 4:4–7)*

The woman at the well was doing a routine chore—drawing water from the well. Nothing was out of the ordinary, except for who was sitting at the well, resting—waiting for her.

I love how the scripture mentions Jesus is tired.

I'm sure He's been exhausted with my own spiritual immaturity, rebellion, and stubbornness at times. But He patiently waits for us.

He wants us to be honest with him about our life. He waits until the perfect time to work things for good or to change us in some way for the better.

2. When we *know* Him—we'll love Him.

> *The Samaritan woman said to him, "You are a Jew and I am a Samaritan woman. How can you ask me for a drink?" (For Jews do not associate with Samaritans.) Jesus answered her, "If you knew the gift of God and who it is that asks you for a drink, you would have asked him and he would have given you living water." (John 4:9–10)*

Jesus doesn't even acknowledge her comment about their differences but goes straight to the heart of the matter.

She doesn't ***know*** Him.

It's one thing to know who Jesus is but it's the real deal when we ***know*** Him in our hearts. Then it's love. I'll never forget figuring out I was "in love" with Jesus. (I didn't even realize we could fall in love with Him. I'd never heard anything about that in the church I grew up in.)

I couldn't stop thinking about Him. For *years.* Everything reminded me of Him, and I saw God in creation everywhere I looked. *Why do I think about God 24/7?*

We think of someone constantly for years and can't get them out of our thoughts because we're **in love**.

When we truly know Jesus, we will love Him.

3. Sometimes, we *don't* believe.

> *"Sir," the woman said, "you have nothing to draw with and the well is deep. Where can you get this living water? Are you greater than our father Jacob, who gave us the well and drank from it himself, as did his sons and his livestock?"*
>
> *Jesus answered, "Everyone who drinks this water will be thirsty again, but whoever drinks the water I give them will never thirst. Indeed, the water I give them will become in them a spring of water welling up to eternal life."*
>
> *The woman said to him, "Sir, give me this water so that I won't get thirsty and have to keep coming here to draw water." (John 4:11–15)*

She must be wondering how something as natural as water can become something that seems impossible. **Living** water? It doesn't make sense.

Jesus is about to transform her natural way of thinking into spiritual drinking.

They're alone when this intimate relationship begins. We may discover our own relationship with Him requires alone time, too.

He works best in us when we're not distracted by the world. Maybe we're in a hospital bed or down on our backs with nothing else but Him to keep us company. It's in these moments, He gets our attention and speaks to our spirit, making His presence known and drawing us close.

4. Jesus opens our eyes to see truth clearly.

> *He told her, "Go, call your husband and come back."*
>
> *"I have no husband," she replied.*
>
> *Jesus said to her, "You are right when you say you have no husband. The fact is, you have had five husbands, and the man you now have is not your husband. What you have just said is quite true."*
>
> *"Sir," the woman said, "I can see that you are a prophet. Our ancestors worshipped on this mountain, but you Jews claim that the place where we must worship is in Jerusalem."*
>
> *"Woman," Jesus replied, "believe me, a time is coming when you will worship the Father neither on this mountain nor in Jerusalem. You Samaritans worship what you do not know;*

> we worship what we do know, for salvation is from the Jews. Yet a time is coming and has now come when the true worshippers will worship the Father in the Spirit and in truth, for they are the kind of worshippers the Father seeks. God is spirit, and his worshippers must worship in the Spirit and in truth."
>
> The woman said, "I know that 'Messiah' (called Christ) is coming. When he comes, he will explain everything to us."
>
> Then Jesus declared, "I, the one speaking to you—I am he." (John 4:16–26)

It didn't take her long to realize Jesus was telling the truth. Her eyes were opened, and His words helped her know Him better.

The same is true for us. It can take a long time to truly get to know someone. He shows us who He is as we go through the troubles of life. We get to know Him better as we go along putting our trust in Him through life's difficulties.

Jesus will replace natural thought with spiritual insight. He takes lies we believe and gives us truth through His word. Helping us worship Him in spirit and in truth.

5. Don't linger in a place you should leave.

> Just then his disciples returned and were surprised to find him talking with a woman. But no one asked, "What do you want?" or "Why are you talking with her?"

> *Then, leaving her water jar, the woman went back to the town and said to the people, "Come, see a man who told me everything I ever did. Could this be the Messiah?" They came out of the town and made their way toward him.*
>
> *Many of the Samaritans from that town believed in him because of the woman's testimony, "He told me everything I ever did." So when the Samaritans came to him, they urged him to stay with them, and he stayed two days. And because of his words many more became believers.*
>
> *They said to the woman, "We no longer believe just because of what you said; now we have heard for ourselves, and we know that this man really is the Savior of the world." (John 4:27–30, 39–42)*

She didn't linger when it was time to leave. Her water jar left behind as evidence of what she forgot about when she met Jesus at the well.

Literally leading others to Jesus with her powerful testimony. They went to Him and asked Jesus to come stay with them. And (my favorite part) because of His **words** many more became believers.

It can be hard to distinguish God's direction when we're not in close relationship with Him.

But when we spend time with Him in prayer, reading the Bible, and surrendered in obedience, we will act out of our personal relationship. We'll want to share what He's done for us with others. We want everyone to know Jesus the way we do.

As Jesus rested by the well, waiting for the woman, He's patiently waiting for us, too.

He knows us quite well even if we don't really **know** Him. He wants to have a heart-to-heart conversation with us as well.

Open your eyes and see Him. **Know** Him. Your heart will never be the same.

***This article was first published 4/3/2022 on Crosswalk.com

• CHAPTER 4 •

Five Life Lessons I Wish I'd Learned before Fifty

I LEARN MOST LIFE lessons the *hard* way.

It might also be true for many others. I can't tell you how many times I've wished I could go back and have a do-over. Now that I've passed up the big five-o, I've learned some lessons I wish I'd learned earlier in life.

There are so many wonderful blessings that come from growing older. Hopefully, being a bit wiser is one of them. Once we reach a certain age, we do seem to look back on our lives. We might wish we'd done a few things differently or at least learned some of those tough life lessons sooner and saved ourselves grief.

We can't go backwards but we can move forward in a better way.

Here are five life lessons I learned after fifty that I wish I'd learned earlier.

1. Listen to Parents

I learned a hard lesson after fifty about taking time to listen to parents.

As children, we don't want to listen to them. We think we know everything especially when we are teenagers. But what they have to say to us is usually tried and true and for our benefit.

Right before Dad became so forgetful in his old age, he wanted to tell me something important. We were visiting my parents in Missouri, sitting in the living room. There were other conversations going on and their wild, little puppy was jumping around all over the place.

I gave Dad my attention and listened to him but was not fully engaged. Mostly, because of the cute puppy but also because of everything else going on in the room.

I was unaware of how serious his forgetfulness actually was because we were living out of state. Nobody knew he had undiagnosed Alzheimer's at that time.

To my dismay, it was the last important conversation we had. He soon began to forget everything.

I wish so desperately I'd pulled up a chair close beside him and given him my full attention. I wish I would have asked him some questions because it was my last chance to have that type of conversation with my dad.

Lesson *learned*.

Listening to parents is not just for kids—it's for grown-ups, too.

> *Honor your father and your mother, as the LORD your God has commanded you, so that you may live long and that it may go well with you in the land the LORD your God is giving you. (Deuteronomy 5:16)*

2. STRESS Less and Trust More

We will have stress in life, that's for sure. But looking back after living over fifty years, I wish I would have stressed *less* over things.

God does allow stress *tests* in our lives in various ways. They can come through financial issues, marital problems, or our own rebellious children. Stress tests are usually about trust. Sometimes they are needed so we *recognize* we aren't trusting God in that area of our lives.

I wish I'd trusted God more in those stressful moments of my younger life instead of worrying and losing sleep.

As we grow as Christians, we trust Him more than we did before. We know He's in control and completely trustworthy.

It would have been best on those restless nights to give it to God and go to sleep.

> *Do not be anxious about anything, but in every situation, by prayer and petition, with thanksgiving, present your requests to God. (Philippians 4:6)*

3. Cherish Dear Friends

We're blessed to have friends as we go through life. We start collecting them when we're very young. Some friendships are short-lived and some last a lifetime.

Truth is, we may only have a *few* dear friends. Those people we can count on for anything. They're there for you in the good times and in the bad times. You truly enjoy their company and miss them when they're gone. Unfortunately, we don't always have as much time with these friends as we'd like.

Last fall we made a trip to Florida and stopped by our dear friend's new house in Georgia along the way. Then later, they took the short drive to our rented beach house and visited with us. We ended our time together eating dinner at a seafood restaurant and planning a possible trip together in the spring of 2020.

Unfortunately, we were never able to take the trip due to COVID-19 and never got to spend any more time with our dear friends in the way we planned.

Instead, we ended up at a funeral just a few weeks ago. One of them passed away suddenly from a brain bleed.

Of course, we're devastated at the loss of our dear friend and can't imagine the world without him. But we're so thankful we took the time on our vacation to find them along the way and visit with them.

Though we have many wonderful memories with our dear friends, I wish we'd made more. Life is short and *dear* friends are few. Make memories with them as often as possible.

A friend loves at all times, and a brother is born for a time of adversity. (Proverbs 17:17)

4. Honor God Even When the Creek Rises . . . .

Growing up Mom said often, "If the good Lord's willing, and the creek don't rise."

Another hard lesson I learned is sometimes the creek *does* rise.

Last year, we received a phone call in the middle of the night from our oldest son. Our daughter-in-law was in labor. The problem was she wasn't due yet. She was twenty-one weeks pregnant with our granddaughter, Nora Jane. They couldn't stop the labor and Nora made an early entrance into the world.

She was born too soon to go to the NICU and be nurtured until she grew big enough to take home. The hospital staff couldn't save her.

She lived almost two hours and I was able to hold her while she was still alive. Holding precious little Nora broke my heart. I wanted her to live. I wanted to bounce her on my knee when she was big enough and I wanted to babysit her. I wanted my granddaughter.

But it wasn't God's will and we were crushed.

It seemed unfair. We could become angry with God over such a thing. But there's purpose even when we don't like it.

We honor God in difficult times by seeking His will in our lives even when it's hard. Even . . . when the creek rises.

The LORD is close to the brokenhearted and saves those who are crushed in spirit. (Psalm 34:18)

5. Enjoy the Ride!

Sometimes, we need to slow down and just enjoy the ride.

We can't go back and relive fifty years of life but we can make our lives better going forward.

My husband and I decided to make our lives more enjoyable a few years ago. We made a big decision and sold our house and bought a cheaper one. We paid off all of our debt except for our smaller mortgage. Then we bought a used pontoon we'd been dreaming of for years.

Our youngest son was growing up fast and the other two had already flown the coop. So, we decided to have more fun while he was still living at home. We'd spent a lot of time working hard just to pay bills and raise our family. It was time for a little more fun.

We've never regretted the boat (yet!) and have enjoyed it thoroughly.

I know not everyone wants a boat. Maybe it's as simple as taking more hikes in nature. Maybe it's more days fishing from the banks of a river. Whatever it is, do things you enjoy as much as possible.

Life is short, but oh how sweet to have a life to live.

Why, you do not even know what will happen tomorrow. What is your life? You are a mist that appears for a little while and then vanishes. (James 4:14)

***This article was first published 9/21/2020 on Crosswalk.com

• CHAPTER 5 •

Seven Marvelous Reasons to Celebrate Having a King

No King.

Those two little words struck me as I studied my Bible one day. I read them several times in the book of Judges. Chapter after chapter, the same phrase appeared.

In those days Israel had no king; everyone did as they saw fit. (Judges 17:6)

In those days Israel had no king. (Judges 18:1)

In those days Israel had no king. (Judges 19:1)

In those days Israel had no king; everyone did as they saw fit. (Judges 21:25)

The definition of *king* according to *Webster's Dictionary* is:

king: *a male monarch of a major territorial unit; especially: one whose position is hereditary and who rules for life*

I was taken aback by the last part *who rules for life*. It means the king rules for as long as *he* lives in this definition. But as Christians, Jesus is our King—He rules our natural and eternal lives. He literally *rules for life.*

To be honest, I'm so thankful to have a King. I'd have a complete mess if I did everything as I saw fit. Who knows where I'd be? The one thing in life I'm confident of is this—there's no other place I'd rather be than surrendered and *following* King Jesus. That much I know.

There are many reasons why we should follow Jesus but with Christmas upon us, here are some marvelous reasons to celebrate having a King.

Here are seven marvelous reasons to celebrate having a King.

1. Jesus is the *PROMISED* King.

Jesus was promised and He keeps His promises.

Have you ever broken a promise? Or has someone you love broken a promise they made to you? It hurts either way and it's disappointing. It does happen sometimes, though. We may try hard to keep a promise, but no matter how hard we try, we end up breaking it. Then we hurt someone and we're disappointed in ourselves.

But Jesus was promised throughout the Old Testament and the New. His birth was foretold and it came to pass. His death was foretold and it came to pass. He does not fail to keep His word. You can trust that.

> *But the angel said to her, "Do not be afraid, Mary; you have found favor with God. You will conceive and give birth to a son, and you are to call him Jesus. He will be great and will be called the Son of the Most High. The Lord God will give him the throne of his father David, and he will reign over Jacob's descendants forever; his kingdom will never end." (Luke 1:30–33)*

2. Jesus is the BORN King.

Jesus was born so that we could be *born again*.

Have you ever held a newborn baby and fell madly in love?

If so, then you can't imagine doing what God did for us. He sent His one and *only* beloved Son to pay the price for our sins. Jesus was born to face death on a cross and to suffer in our place. Can you imagine that kind of love?

He came to save us. When we recognize our need of Him and follow Him, putting our faith completely in Him, we are **born *again***.

Through Him, we have eternal life in heaven. Without Him, we are lost.

> *For God so loved the world, that he gave his one and only Son, that whoever believes in him shall not perish but have eternal life. (John 3:16)*

3. Jesus is the *COME TO ME* King.

Kings in history have often said, "Off with their head!"

But Jesus says, "Come to me," instead.

A king who asks us to come to Him? It's unheard of. There's a lot of red tape to get to speak to a king. Your chances of speaking to any king, even in this day and age, are slim to none. (It's probably not going to happen.) But Jesus invites us, "Come to me."

How marvelous!

We celebrate a King who *wants* to hear from us. He wants us to share what's on our hearts with Him. He wants to help us and give us rest. He desires a relationship with you and me.

> *"Come to me, all you who are weary and burdened, and I will give you rest."* (Matthew 11:28)

4. Jesus is the WALKING WITH US King.

Jesus walked a mile in our shoes.

Jesus (fully God and fully man) lived a perfect life on earth without sinning. Because He walked in our shoes, He understands our struggles. He relates to our sufferings and empathizes with us.

Generally, a king is raised in a royal household. He has servants and doesn't do manual labor.

Jesus left His royal home to live a humble life and He worked with His hands as a carpenter.

This is **not** your average king.

> *In the beginning was the Word, and the Word was with God, and the Word was God. (John 1:1) The Word became flesh and made his dwelling among us. We have seen his glory, the glory of the one and only Son, who came from the Father, full of grace and truth. (John 1:14)*

5. Jesus is the *I GOT YOU* King.

"*I got you.*" Have you heard someone say that to you in response to a need?

I doubt you'd ever hear it coming from a king. Have you ever heard of a king who is loyal to you? Most kings expect loyalty but may not return the favor. They might throw you into prison or a dungeon. But we have the King who won't turn on us.

As a matter of fact, when we are in Christ, He has us in the palm of His hand. He won't let go. And nobody can take us from Him.

He's got us.

> *I give them eternal life, and they shall never perish; no one will snatch them out of my hand. (John 10:28) My Father, who has given them to me, is greater than all; no one can snatch them out of my Father's hand. (John 10:29)*

6. Jesus is the *ROCK BOTTOM* King.

When we're at the end of our rope and we hit rock bottom, Jesus is the **Rock** at the bottom.

Usually, we exhaust ourselves from our own efforts before we finally turn to Jesus for help. He's there at rock bottom (whatever that may be) waiting patiently for us to give Him our problems and let go. He will handle it. Trust Him.

We take refuge in the shelter that is Jesus Christ, our Rock.

> *But the LORD has become my fortress, and my God the rock in whom I take refuge. (Psalm 94:22)*

7. Jesus is the *KING OF KINGS*.

There is NO other king like Him.

Instead of condemning us to die for our own sins, He died for them instead. He made a way for us so that we can live.

He has *our* best interest at heart each and every moment of our lives. He will do what He says He will do and **keeps** His promises.

There's no other king who deserves our trust and loyalty more. We can never say "Thank you!" enough.

***This article was first published 12/11/2019 on Crosswalk.com

• CHAPTER 6 •

Seven Prayers for Christmas Dinner to Renew the Hearts of Everyone Present

CHRISTMAS IS A BEAUTIFUL thing.

A time for us to celebrate the birth of our promised savior. We thank God for His goodness and His perfect plan of salvation. Families gather with joyful hearts to share a lovely dinner.

This is what Christmas should be . . . but let's get *real*.

Christmas can be stressful. There's a big meal to prepare and desserts to make. We busy ourselves baking Christmas cookies and making decadent candies.

We have church programs, caroling, and choir performances. Along with office parties, neighborhood gatherings, and various dinners to attend.

We shop 'til we drop buying gifts, decorations, and stocking stuffers. There's online shopping, sales, and home deliveries to keep in mind.

Finally, we wrap presents and hope everyone will be happy with the gifts we purchased. Then we find ourselves double guessing everything we bought. *Maybe I should give a gift card to a favorite store instead?* Or even worse, we worry . . . *Did I buy enough?*

We get so wrapped up in the holiday STUFF we forget why we're celebrating. Instead of growing closer to Jesus, we can find ourselves farther away.

How can we *renew our hearts* this time of year?

Here are seven prayers for Christmas dinner to renew the hearts of everyone present.

1. The *Grateful Hearts* Prayer

> *Gracious Father,*
>
> *Thank you for all you've given to us. We're thankful for each family member and friend gathered here today.*
>
> *Sometimes we grow tired and become unthankful. Help us to have gratitude for the good things in our lives. But also, for the things that are not-so-good because we know You work all things together for our good.*
>
> *Father, bless this food and bless those who have prepared it. May it nourish our bodies and strengthen us.*

In the powerful name of Jesus, Amen.

And we know that in all things God works for the good of those who love him, who have been called according to his purpose. (Romans 8:28)

2. The *Unspoken* Prayer

Heavenly Father,

Thank you for this day and for those gathered together for Christmas. Thank you for this food and fellowship with friends and family.

Some of us come to You with heavy hearts from carrying the burdens of life. We lift unspoken prayers to You today. If it be Your will, work in a powerful way. Help us recognize the answers You give and to see Your work clearly in our lives.

Thank you, in advance, for answering unspoken prayers.

In Jesus' powerful name, Amen.

Therefore I tell you, whatever you ask for in prayer, believe that you have received it, and it will be yours. (Mark 11:24)

3. The *Presence* Prayer

Heavenly Father,

*As we gather to celebrate the birth of Your Son, we thank You for sending us the best gift ever—**Jesus**. We praise You for Your perfect plan to make things right. While we struggle at times to give good presents to each other, You gave the perfect gift that only You could give.*

Thank you for the presence of every person gathered here today for Christmas dinner. We're thankful for every family member and friend around this table. Each is special in their own way. Bless each one.

Thank you for your provision and bless the food before us.

In the sweet name of Jesus, Amen.

For God so loved the world, that he gave his one and only Son, that whoever believes in him should not perish but have eternal life. (John 3:16)

4. The *Sin-LESS* Prayer

Heavenly Father,

We can't say "thank you" enough for all that you've done for us. You sent Your Son to save us. He lived a perfect, sinless life and died a terrible death on the cross bearing the weight of all our sins.

We're incapable of living a sinless life. But help us to sin LESS. Show us our sin through the power of the Holy

Spirit. Help us to recognize it and turn away from whatever it may be. Make the unknown sins known to us so that we can be a little more like Jesus.

In His powerful, mighty name we pray, Amen.

For all have sinned and fall short of the glory of God. (Romans 3:23)

5. The *Anyway* Prayer

Heavenly Father,

Thank you for loving us in such a wonderful way. It's beyond our comprehension.

Help us to love each other the way You love us. Most times our love for each other is pretty "iffy" based on good behavior or expectations. Help us to love "even if" instead.

***Your** love toward us is perfect. It's unconditional, deep love. It's true and overflows with grace and mercy. Even though we've all disappointed you on every level, You love us anyway.*

My command is this: Love each other as I have loved you. (John 15:12)

6. The *Fresh Starts and Forgiving Hearts* Prayer

Heavenly Father,

We've all made mistakes. Thank you for giving us a fresh start through forgiveness. We want to forgive and be forgiven by others not only with words but with hearts as well.

If we're holding onto anger or have a grudge against another, help us to let go and put it behind us. If we've hurt someone, help us right the wrong by asking them for forgiveness.

We want to love and forgive others as You love and forgive us. This Christmas, help us move forward with a fresh start and forgiving hearts.

In Jesus' name, Amen.

"Therefore, if you are offering your gift at the altar and there remember that your brother or sister has something against you, leave your gift there in front of the altar. First go and be reconciled to them; then come and offer your gift. (Matthew 5:23–24)

7. The *Gifts* Prayer

Heavenly Father,

Thank you for giving good gifts.

Jesus came to die so we can live. What a gift!

He did something wonderful. We want to do good things, too. Help us to put our thoughts on others.

Bring to mind those we know who might be hurting or struggling this Christmas. Compel us to do something kind for them. No questions asked. No strings attached. Just because it's Christmas.

In the mighty and powerful name of Jesus, Amen.

***This article was first published 11/4/2019 on Crosswalk.com

• CHAPTER 7 •

How Would Jesus Respond to Beggars?

HAVE YOU EVER IGNORED a beggar?

To be honest, I have. It can be annoying to see the same person on the street each day holding a sign as if that's *their* full-time job as we drive by, heading to a job we don't even like.

But sometimes life is hard and things don't go our way. It can happen to anyone given the right circumstances. We could develop serious health problems, drug addiction, mental illness, job loss, etc. We could end up homeless, penniless, and possibly begging.

When my youngest son was a baby we were barely scraping by each month. I stayed home with him and my husband drove a truck for a living. Each week, after I deposited his paycheck, I'd head to the store to buy household necessities.

This particular day, I made the deposit and kept twenty-eight dollars in cash and put it in my wallet. It was for anything that came up until the next payday. Not a lot of cash for a whole week but I'd make it work.

As I drove to the store with baby in tow and pulled off the exit, I groaned. There was the homeless man with his sign again, asking for help. Usually, I got lucky and the light would be green so I'd just drive on by. But this day I was the first car to stop at the red light and the beggar stood inches from my car.

I don't know why I did it but instead of ignoring him, I turned and faced him. Deep lines in his face conveyed he'd lived a rough life. The moment our eyes met, I felt a nudge to give him money but thought, *I don't even know how much to give.* God spoke clearly to my spirit. *Give him the five dollar bill in your wallet.*

I pulled the five from my wallet, rolled down the window, and handed him the money. His cold hand brushed mine as he took it and said, "God bless you."

"God bless you, too." I rolled up the window as the light turned green and drove to the store, overcome with emotion.

After I finished shopping, I drove back toward the interstate. I saw the homeless man walking away from a fast-food restaurant. I smiled. *I guess God wanted to feed him breakfast.*

My thoughts toward giving money to homeless people changed that day. I will give when prompted by God to give. Because yes, there are some out there who beg as a full-time job and probably make more money doing that than working somewhere. They may spend it on alcohol or drugs. We have to be cautious but seek God and be *obedient*.

As Christians, we should try to model the behavior of our Savior. We've been given a great example to follow.

Here are three wonderful responses from Jesus in Luke 18:35–43.

1. Jesus listens to the beggar who called out to Him in his trouble.

> *As Jesus approached Jericho, a blind man was sitting by the roadside begging. When he heard the crowd going by, he asked what was happening. They told him, "Jesus of Nazareth is passing by." He called out, "Jesus, Son of David, have mercy on me!" Those who led the way rebuked him and told him to be quiet, but he shouted all the more, "Son of David, have mercy on me!" (Luke 18:35–39)*

The blind beggar finds out Jesus is passing by and calls out for mercy. When he was rebuked and told to be quiet, he shouted all the **more**. He *knew* Jesus and what He could do for him. He had to or why would he persist in asking for mercy? He showed great faith by continuing to call out for Jesus even when he was told to be quiet. He didn't want to miss his opportunity. Jesus *heard* him and responded.

We, too, can listen. When we see someone begging, we should listen to the Holy Spirit. Is He telling us to give or not?

2. Jesus shows compassion and mercy.

> *Jesus stopped and ordered the man to be brought to him. When he came near, Jesus asked him, "What do you want me to do for you?"*

"Lord, I want to see," he replied. *(Luke 18:40–41)*

When the beggar called out, Jesus heard him and stopped. Then Jesus **ordered** the man to be brought to Him. The beggar is brought before the King. Jesus shows compassion and mercy toward him by stopping and then asking, "What do you want Me to do for you?"

Like Jesus, we should show compassion. Whether we give money or not, we should be kind. We can offer a warm smile and a kind greeting if nothing else. Our tendency is to ignore and I'm as guilty as the next person but everyone deserves kindness and acknowledgment in some form.

3. Jesus gives what is needed.

> *Jesus said to him, "Receive your sight; your faith has healed you." Immediately he received his sight and followed Jesus, praising God. When all the people saw it, they also praised God. (Luke 18:42–43)*

If God speaks to us and nudges us to give money, by all means, *obey* God. We have no idea why God wants to give that particular person money. He may just want to feed him breakfast. He may want the beggar to know He is listening, has compassion, and wants to give him what's needed at that moment.

We see a domino effect in this passage with spiritual implications. After the beggar received his sight, he *followed* Jesus, praising God. Then *everyone* who saw it, praised God, too. This makes my soul *dance*.

God wants to use us in the life of another person and that's quite an honor.

Four Scriptures about the Poor

> *"Whoever is kind to the poor lends to the LORD, and he will reward them for what they have done." (Proverbs 19:17)*

> *But as for me, I am poor and needy; may the LORD think of me. You are my help and my deliverer; you are my God, do not delay. (Psalm 40:17)*

> *The poor you will always have with you, but you will not always have me. (Matthew 26:11)*

> *The poor plead for mercy, but the rich answer harshly. (Proverbs 18:23)*

It can be easy to pass judgment on a person begging beside a road. Especially, if they have pets with them or children. Some unscrupulous people will use pretty much anything to get a person to feel sorry for them and give them money.

But we need to seek God and be *obedient*. He's faithful to answer about when to give and when to withhold.

The truth is, we're all *beggars* in desperate need of Jesus. God didn't ignore us. He didn't withhold what we need the most. He showed compassion and ***gave*** His beloved Son for us.

For God so loved the world that he gave his one and only Son, that whoever believes in him shall not perish but have eternal life. (John 3:16)

So, how would Jesus respond to beggars?

With compassion, mercy, and great *love*.

***This article was first published 7/1/2020 on Crosswalk.com

• CHAPTER 8 •

Books of the Bible Every Senior Should Study

Most people love a good book.

We can be swept away in a story full of intrigue, betrayal, murder, and perfect twists. Then the ending fulfills every promise made by the author. We finish and can't wait to tell everyone else what a great book it was and recommend they read it, too.

If you've never read the Bible—you're missing out. There's more than one reason it's referred to as the "Good Book."

It really is a *good* book. It has it all and then some more—a rollercoaster ride for the soul. You'll find the inside scoop to many questions we have in life.

- Where did we come from?
- Why are we the way we are?
- What is love?
- Why do I feel something is missing?

It's thick and can be a bit intimidating. But isn't it awesome we have the opportunity to *know* the author of the best-selling book of **all** time?

When we read the Bible, we're getting to know God. His Word is alive and changes us when we read it.

> *For the word of God is alive and active. Sharper than any double-edged sword, it penetrates even to dividing soul and spirit, joints and marrow; it judges the thoughts and attitudes of the heart. (Hebrews 4:12)*

My own thoughts about God have changed as I recognized what I *thought* wasn't true. The Bible can transform us and trade the lies we might believe for truth.

> *All scripture is God-breathed and is useful for teaching, rebuking, correcting and training in righteousness. (2 Timothy 3:16)*

We have the greatest story of all time written down for each of us to know what God really thinks about things. And how He feels about us.

Reading it is *wonderful* but when we study, we will find invaluable treasure.

Here are five books of the Bible every senior should study.

1. Genesis

So many incredible events take place in the book of Genesis:

- Creation
- The first sin and a curse
- The first murder
- God floods the earth
- Joseph and a great famine

When we read through Genesis or remember the stories from when we were young, we get great information. But when we take time to study the events and what God does throughout this book, we see Jesus coming at the very beginning of the Bible. Foreshadowed wonderfully for us to find in the pages of this book.

He's shown when God speaks to the serpent while casting down the curse in Genesis.

> *And I will put enmity between you and the woman and between your offspring and hers; he will crush your head, and you will strike his heel." (Genesis 3:15)*

God makes clothes to cover Adam and Eve when they recognize their nakedness. It's the first animal sacrifice and it's to cover them because of their sin of disobedience.

> *The LORD God made garments of skin for Adam and his wife and clothed them. (Genesis 3:21)*

Jesus' sacrifice on the cross later is the ultimate covering for each of us. There are so many incredible ways to see Jesus in the book of Genesis. God already had His plan for us set in motion.

2. Job

If you've been a Christian for any length of time, you've probably had to deal with the devil. This is the book to study if you ponder such things.

> *One day the angels came to present themselves before the LORD, and Satan also came with them. The LORD said to Satan, "Where have you come from?"*
>
> *Satan answered the LORD, "From roaming throughout the earth, going back and forth on it."*
>
> *Then the LORD said to Satan, "Have you considered my servant Job? There is no one on earth like him; he is blameless and upright, a man who fears God and shuns evil." (Job 1:6–8)*

Just reading Job is eye-opening. We get a glimpse of what God *will* allow in our lives. If we read carefully, we see God didn't make bad things happen to Job but He did allow them. The same is true with us.

We clearly see Satan's desire to cause us as much grief as possible in our lives. He wants to find ways to turn us against God.

The first time I read this book, I read the entire thing in one sitting. Talk about a *good* read. But how much more will we find if we take the time to study it?

3. Daniel

I love this book.

We remember Daniel most because of the story found here about Daniel and the lion's den. We know him for his bravery, obedience, and trust in God.

But if we study this book a bit, we learn so much more. The dreams, visions, and prophecies are intriguing.

It's amazing how God worked through him and gave him not only the meaning of the king's dream but showed Daniel the **actual** dream, too. His life and the lives of others, depended on it.

Only God could have shown him the dream of another person. Incredible.

> *The king said to Daniel, "Surely your God is the God of gods and the Lord of kings and a revealer of mysteries, for you were able to reveal this mystery." (Daniel 2:47)*

4. John

The Gospel of John brings everything together and ties it up neatly with a bow. Like any well-written book, the first sentence is captivating.

> *In the beginning was the Word, and the Word was with God, and the Word was God. (John 1:1)*

Jesus revealed from the very beginning.

> *The Word became flesh and made his dwelling among us. We have seen his glory, the glory of the one and only Son, who came from the Father, full of grace and truth. (John 1:14)*

When I fell in love with Jesus, I soaked up the New Testament. I couldn't get enough of the Gospels because they told the story of Jesus. They are *beautiful*. Well worth taking the time to study.

5. Revelation

Studying the book of Revelation is on my list for this year. I've read it but have not done an actual study. It's interesting yet also intimidating with so much symbolism.

After managing to get through 2020, many are turning to the Bible for guidance for end times. Most of us have never quite experienced such upheaval in our lives like we did last year. Now, we understand a little better what the end time may be like.

We're much better off knowing exactly what the symbolism in Revelation means and how it will all play out.

> *Blessed is the one who reads aloud the words of this prophecy, and blessed are those who hear it and take to heart what is written in it, because the time is near. (Revelation 1:3)*

Sometimes, we just need a few words of peace and comfort from the Bible. If you're seeking comfort then head to the book of Psalms.

At times, I camp out there. Especially, if I'm struggling through a difficult time in life where nothing is going right.

Whether we're hurt, distressed, or at a loss with life in general, the beautiful words in Psalms ground us. We're *reminded* God is faithful and we know everything will be alright.

> *As for God, his way is perfect: The Lord's word is flawless; he shields all who take refuge in him. (Psalm 19:3)*

***This article was first published 6/28/2021 on Crosswalk.com

• CHAPTER 9 •

A Comforting Prayer for Miscarriages

MOST OF US BEGIN loving a child the moment we discover we're pregnant.

The love grows as the child grows within us. We dream about what they will look like and whether they'll be a boy or a girl. We may already have a name in mind for them before they're even conceived.

The love grows deeper with each passing day. We think of them constantly and fall deeply in love. If there is a miscarriage and we lose the baby, it can be devastating. Because we loved this little person even though we hadn't gotten the chance to meet them yet.

With deep loves comes deep grief. Our hearts break because the one we loved is gone. The day we longed for where we'd hold them in our arms and count fingers and toes and celebrate their birth is gone. It can be difficult to understand.

When I lost a baby at six weeks of pregnancy, I was hurt but also angry. I wanted the baby so much and didn't understand why God allowed a miscarriage. It didn't seem fair. Of course, I was spiritually immature at this time and threw a temper tantrum like a spoiled toddler might do in the grocery store. I didn't talk to God for a couple of weeks.

More recently, my daughter-in-law went into labor at twenty-one weeks and gave premature birth to our sweet granddaughter, Nora. She lived nearly two hours but couldn't survive at that stage. The deep grief was crushing because we were madly in love with her. An ultrasound photo a couple weeks earlier captured a big smile and a wave. Precious.

We were able to hold Nora before she passed away. Holding her and knowing she wouldn't survive was a horrible experience. She was perfectly healthy. Just born too soon.

Why would God give and then take away?

We may never know the answer until we get to heaven but while we're in this fallen world, we'll experience loss, including the loss of our most beloved little ones. Whether a miscarriage or a birth where the child is unable to survive on its own, it's a sad part of life.

Though he brings grief, he will show compassion, so great is his unfailing love. For he does not willingly bring affliction or grief to anyone. (Lamentations 3:32–33)

It can be difficult to know what to say to someone who has just lost a baby. Here are a few thoughts from those of us who have experienced pregnancy or infant loss.

What to Say to Someone Who Has Had a Miscarriage

It's best to express sympathy with simple words.

- "This is terrible and I'm so sorry."
- "I'm sorry for what you're going through."
- "I know this hurts. I'm praying for you."
- "Please know I'm here if you need to talk."

What *Not* to Say to Someone Who Has Had a Miscarriage

Don't try to assign reason or explain things. Someone in deep grief doesn't want to hear explanations unless they're from their doctor about why they lost their child. They need to know others care about what they're going through not that they might know why it happened.

Try to ***avoid*** saying these statements.

- "Everything happens for a reason."
- "God won't give more than you can handle."
- "You're still young. There's plenty of time to have children."
- "I can't imagine what you're going through."
- "God knows what He's doing."
- "There was probably something wrong with it or it was probably for the best."

Actions Can Speak Louder than Words

- Make an effort to show sympathy by attending the funeral (if there is one).
- Make yourself available in some other way. This can be powerful for the grieving parent.
- Allow the loss parent to share their story if they're comfortable doing so in their own time.

Comforting Bible Verses for Miscarriages

> *As you do not know the path of the wind, or how the body is formed in a mother's womb, so you cannot understand the work of God, the Maker of all things. (Ecclesiastes 11:5)*

And my God will meet all your needs according to the riches of his glory in Christ Jesus. (Philippians 4:19)

> *God is our refuge and strength, an ever-present help in trouble. Therefore we will not fear, though the earth give way and the mountains fall into the heart of the sea, though its waters roar and foam and the mountains quake with their surging. (Psalm 46 1:3)*

> *Before I formed you in the womb I knew you, before you were born I set you apart; I appointed you as a prophet to the nations. (Jeremiah 1:5)*

> *For you created my inmost being; you knit me together in my mother's womb. I praise you because I am fearfully and*

wonderfully made; your works are wonderful, I know that full well. My frame was not hidden from you when I was made in the secret place, when I was woven together in the depths of the earth. Your eyes saw my unformed body; all the days ordained for me were written in your book before one of them came to be. (Psalm 139:13–16)

Jesus said, "Let the little children come to me, and do not hinder them, for the kingdom of heaven belongs to such as these." (Matthew 19:14)

Prayer for Miscarriage: A Prayer for the Parents

Heavenly Father,

Thank you for the parents of this precious baby. Heal their broken hearts and strengthen their faith through this storm. Help them find comfort not only in Your word but in the words of friends or family who've experienced the same pain. Draw them closer to You through this tragedy and reveal Yourself to them in their time of need.

In the powerful name of Jesus, Amen.

"I have told you these things, so that in me you may have peace. In this world you will have trouble. But take heart! I have overcome the world." (John 16:33)

Prayer for Miscarriage: A Prayer for the Family

Heavenly Father,

Thank you for being with us during this devastating time. Our hearts are crushed. We don't understand why we've lost this child. But we trust You to get us through it.

In the mighty and powerful name of Jesus, Amen.

The LORD is close to the brokenhearted and saves those who are crushed in spirit (Psalm 34:18)

Prayer for Miscarriage: A Prayer for the Baby

Father,

Thank you for this precious little one. Though our hopes for this child's life were not realized, we know You're in control of everything. Your thoughts are not our thoughts and Your ways are not our ways. It's hard for us to understand but we know our sweet baby is with You in heaven and one day we will be able to meet her face-to-face. We look forward to the time we can hold her in our arms and give her the love we've longed so deeply to give.

In the name of Jesus, Amen.

"For my thoughts are not your thoughts, neither are your ways my ways," declares the LORD. "As the heavens are

higher than the earth, so are my ways higher than your ways and my thoughts than your thoughts. (Isaiah 55:8–9)

***This article was first published 8/12/2021 on Crosswalk.com

• CHAPTER 10 •

Four Ways Jesus Calms the Storms in Our Lives

SOMETIMES, IT TAKES A storm to get our attention.

Maybe not a literal hurricane but a storm of life. We've lost our job. We've lost someone we love deeply. Maybe we've lost *hope*. It's then we cry out to Jesus for help. Disaster has fallen upon us, and we *need* Him.

It seems to be these times in life when we recognize our desperate need for a Savior. Someone to make everything right again. Someone to grab hold of us and pull us from the turbulent water sucking us into its murky depths. Someone to save us.

Often, Jesus comes to our rescue like He did for the disciples who were caught in a boat rocking in the waves of a lake during a violent storm.

> *That day when evening came, he said to his disciples, "Let us go over to the other side." Leaving the crowd behind, they*

took him along, just as he was, in the boat. There were also other boats with him. A furious squall came up, and the waves broke over the boat, so that it was nearly swamped. Jesus was in the stern, sleeping on a cushion. The disciples woke him and said to him, "Teacher, don't you care if we drown?"

He got up, rebuked the wind and said to the waves, "Quiet! Be still!" Then the wind died down and it was completely calm.

He said to his disciples, "Why are you so afraid? Do you still have no faith?"

They were terrified and asked each other, "Who is this? Even the wind and the waves obey him!" (Mark 4:35–41)

What Do We Learn from the Story of When Jesus Calms the Storm in the Bible?

If we read the whole story in Mark from the beginning of chapter 4, we'll notice Jesus doing a lot of teaching. There are so many there beside the lake listening, so He gets into the boat to teach the crowd from there.

Then, in the evening, they set out to go to the other side of the lake and encounter the storm. Jesus is asleep and unconcerned with the weather. He's resting but also *testing*. We know this because of His response to the disciples' fear and their lack of faith.

In the next chapter, some awesome miracles take place *after* the storm. When they reach the other side of the lake, Jesus casts out a legion of demons from a man. Then they cross the lake again and Jesus heals the woman who touches his garment and raises a dead girl to life. The disciples witness these miracles.

What happened with the disciples in these chapters is often the same with us spiritually.

We may go through a season of teaching from Jesus, then testing as the life storm comes our way; then, on the other side of it, we may see Jesus do something astounding or miraculous in our own lives.

There's teaching, a *trust* test, and then triumph.

Why We Can Trust Jesus When Storms Come

To be honest, when we're a new Christian, it can be scary facing a storm in life and not knowing how to handle it. We may question God's love for us. We might question why He'd allow us to go through such a difficult time. We may waiver in our faith.

But if we've been a Christian for a long time, He has proven Himself *trustworthy* through many of life's storms.

The storms make us stronger and build a deeper level of trust in Jesus. He does not fail us even if He doesn't stop the wind and waves as He did for the disciples on the lake.

Sometimes, we must ride it out with Him by our side. He's with us through it all. He has purpose in everything He allows, and we trust Him to get us through it.

> *The LORD himself goes before you and will be with you; he will never leave you nor forsake you. Do not be afraid; do not be discouraged." (Deuteronomy 31:8)*

Four Ways Jesus Calms the Storm in Our Lives

1. Jesus is with us in the storms of life.

Having a friend who goes with us through dark times is priceless. We are not alone during our darkest hour. He's with us. He never leaves us or forsakes us when it seems the everyone else has let us down.

> *Fear not, for I am with you; do not be dismayed, for I am your God. I will strengthen you and help you; I will uphold you with my righteous right hand. (Isaiah 41:10)*

2. Jesus is light in the dark storm.

Sometimes, there's a break in the bad weather like the eye of a hurricane. A brief time where the storm lightens up and we gather the strength to make it through what remains of the storm.

We can find peace to get us through by reading God's Word. Jesus is the Word and does wonders for our souls when we're being hit by strong wind and rain. Whether we're reading the words of Jesus in the Gospels or seeking solace in the Psalms. Our souls are strengthened through the Word of God.

> *Your word is a lamp for my feet, a light on my path. (Psalm 119:105)*

3. Jesus calms the storm in our lives through prayer.

Our instinct is to tell someone our troubles when we go through a difficult time in life. It helps to get everything off our chest.

Jesus is our best friend. He's listening to us even when we can only groan in our spirits because we don't have words to express our deep sorrow. He already knows everything we're going through but humbling ourselves and seeking Him is the best way to calm our spirits.

> *May my prayer be set before you like incense; may the lifting up of my hands be like the evening sacrifice. (Psalm 141:2)*

4. Jesus calms the storm in our lives through other Christians.

When we're part of a church family and a storm of life comes along, we have prayer warriors seeking God on our behalf. They're concerned about what we're going through and praying for our well-being.

God speaks through other Christians, at times, when we need it most. It's wise to seek counsel from another older Christian who has been there, done that. Their advice is tested and true. They can bring comfort to us and calm our souls.

God knows when the storm of life is coming our way. Nothing catches Him by surprise. He's in control and can stop the storm if He chooses. But most often, He allows it. There's something to be gained spiritually from going through a storm. It can be painful, but we rarely grow without a little pain.

We become compassionate for what others go through when we've ridden those same waves of trouble ourselves. We understand things we never understood before and realize it could be any one of us in the situation.

The truth is life storms most often *soften* our hearts, make us humble, and make us more like Jesus.

> *"All this I have spoken while still with you. But the Advocate, the Holy Spirit, whom the Father will send in my name, will teach you all things and will remind you of everything I have said to you. Peace I leave with you; my peace I give you. I do not give to you as the world gives. Do not let your hearts be troubled and do not be afraid. (John 14:25–27)*

***This article was first published 9/27/2021 on Crosswalk.com

• CHAPTER 11 •

How to See What God Sees in You in a Culture of Filters and Facebook Highlights

One rainy day, my husband came home from work, and I met him on the back porch. The rain had just stopped, and sunshine poured across the yard.

"Is there a rainbow?"

"Yep." He pointed in the direction of our neighbor's house. A rainbow lit up the sky above their home.

"It's not very bright," I said.

We both pulled out our phones and snapped pictures. Then he looked at me with a sly grin before we stepped inside the house and said, "You do realize you just complained about a rainbow."

Yikes. The realization stopped me in my tracks. He was right. I complained. How in the world could I find fault with a rainbow? And *why* did I find fault?

I pondered my complaint all evening. Finally, it dawned on me why I thought it wasn't quite bright enough. I had compared it to another rainbow.

A few years back, we saw the most beautiful, double rainbow by our house and it seemed to end right in our own backyard. I'd never seen anything like it in my life. It was the grandest rainbow ever.

But just because I'd seen a brighter, more magnificent one didn't diminish the fact that God gave another rainbow for all to enjoy. It was probably bigger and brighter to someone else and maybe it landed in their backyard, too.

God made me aware of an issue with my spirit through a rainbow revelation. I realized some of my complaints are born from comparison. When I saw the rainbow over my neighbor's house and it wasn't quite as bright as the rainbow I'd seen before, I complained about it.

Comparing rainbows, or ourselves in all areas, is a terrible trap. It's made worse by social media. Using filters is commonplace these days. They are built-in on Instagram. Our phones allow pictures to be filtered before posting them to Facebook.

It's easy to compare ourselves or our lives with those who are putting their best foot forward using fancy filters to make themselves look better in every possible way.

I'm not going to lie. I love a good filter. *Ha!* It's fun to snap silly pictures with family and friends using different types of filters.

But it's not so fun when we find ourselves complaining because we've compared ourselves to someone else and we begin to find fault.

- *They're happier than I am.*
- *They're more attractive than I am.*
- *They look ten years younger than they are and when I look in the mirror, I see wrinkles and age spots already.*

Comparison can steal our happiness, self-worth, and joy. It can dull the brightness of what God has given to us. If you've found yourself falling into the comparison trap or doubting your worth, **here are a few ways to see what God sees in you.**

1. God sees a treasure.

When we find fault through comparison and complain about ourselves, our self-esteem can go right down the toilet. But no matter how down we get on ourselves, know that God considers His children to be a *treasured* possession. Our life is a precious gift.

We are His and He loves us like no one else ever will. **You are treasured.**

> *And the Lord has declared this day that you are his people, his treasured possession as he promised, and that you are to keep all his commands. (Deuteronomy 26:18)*

2. God sees a wonderful creation.

It's easy to pick out our own flaws. We live in our bodies so long that we start to get on our own nerves.

We may not like a particular feature on our face or maybe we hate how our second toe is longer than our big toe. Everyone has something they wish they could change but God made us wonderfully. No one else is like you.

You may see flaws, but God sees His lovely creation. Embrace that second toe and show it some love. God made it and He knows what He's doing.

God's works are wonderful and you are, too.

> *I praise you because I am fearfully and wonderfully made; your works are wonderful; I know that full well. (Psalm 139:14)*

3. God sees someone He delights in.

When we're disappointed in ourselves, we feel anything but delighted. Maybe we don't get to church as often as we'd like. Maybe we lost our job or disappointed someone we love. It happens and usually at the worst possible time.

But we have a creator who knows we're not perfect. He actually *delights* in us. Another way to say delight is *great pleasure*. He takes great pleasure in us.

The Lord delights in those who fear him, who put their hope in his unfailing love. (Psalm 147:11)

4. God sees an overcomer.

Most everyone loves to use a good filter because we want to look better than we really are.

Spiritually, Jesus is the best filter ever and makes us better than we could ever be on our own. Through Him, we are made right with God. Through Him, we can do all things because He gives us strength. Through Him, our sins are as far away from us as the East is from the West.

We can overcome whatever shortfalls or issues we deal with in life through Him.

You, dear children, are from God and have overcome them, because the one who is in you is greater than the one who is in the world. (1 John 4:4)

5. God sees you protected.

With Jesus in our heart, we have God on our side.

That doesn't mean we won't have trouble, or we won't feel afraid at times. But we have a great defender and protector.

You are my hiding place; you will protect me from trouble and surround me with songs of deliverance. (Psalm 32:7)

6. God sees a deeply loved child.

Let's face it. Social media is shallow. People hit like without even reading what you've written or they withhold their like for no reason at all. Though it's fun and everyone is doing it, we can never count our self-worth by how many likes or shares our post or photo receives.

It almost seems clichéd to say, "God loves you." But it's **so true.** We can't even comprehend His deep love for us. It's a beautiful thing. **You are deeply loved.**

> *But God demonstrates His own love for us in this: While we were still sinners, Christ died for us. (Romans 5:8)*

7. God sees blessed.

It's hard to feel confident when we've compared ourselves to someone else and we begin to feel insecure. But when we lack confidence in ourselves, we can trust God and have confidence in Him. We're blessed when we trust God and He's completely trustworthy. **You are blessed.**

> *"But blessed is the one who trusts in the LORD, whose confidence is in him. (Jeremiah 17:7)*

If you've felt the sting of comparison, as many have, take a look at yourself through the filter of Jesus Christ and know that God sees you as treasured, wonderfully made, delightful, an overcomer, protected, deeply loved and blessed.

"As the Father has loved me, so have I loved you. Now remain in my love. (John 15:9)

***This article was first published 1/20/2020 on Crosswalk.com

• CHAPTER 12 •

Three Lessons We Can Learn from Moses' Wife Zipporah

THE WIFE OF MOSES is named Zipporah. There's not a lot mentioned about her in the Bible. However, she's known for one major thing and it's a bit strange.

She circumcised her son with a flint knife to save Moses because God was going to *kill* him.

Zipporah's father, Jethro, was a priest in the land of Midian where Moses fled after killing an Egyptian. Jethro had given Zipporah to Moses as his wife. They had two sons before Moses had the burning bush experience and was called by God to go to Egypt so the children of Israel would be set free from bondage.

At the time of the odd scene, Moses was on his way to Egypt as instructed by God to speak to Pharaoh, so he'd let the Israelites go. They'd been in slavery for 430 years. (Exodus 12:40)

The interesting event involving Zipporah is found in Exodus, chapter 4:

> Then Moses went back to Jethro his father-in-law and said to him, "Let me return to my own people in Egypt to see if any of them are still alive." Jethro said, "Go, and I wish you well."
>
> Now the LORD had said to Moses in Midian, "Go back to Egypt, for all those who wanted to kill you are dead." So Moses took his wife and sons, put them on a donkey and started back to Egypt. And he took the staff of God in his hand.
>
> The LORD said to Moses, "When you return to Egypt, see that you perform before Pharaoh all the wonders I have given you the power to do. But I will harden his heart so that he will not let the people go. Then say to Pharaoh, 'This is what the LORD says: Israel is my firstborn son, and I told you, "Let my son go, so he may worship me." But you refused to let him go; so I will kill your firstborn son.'"
>
> At a lodging place on the way, the LORD met Moses and was about to kill him. But Zipporah took a flint knife, cut off her son's foreskin and touched Moses' feet with it. "Surely you are a bridegroom of blood to me," she said. So, the LORD let him alone. (At that time she said "bridegroom of blood," referring to circumcision.) (Exodus 4:18–26)

The scripture is sort of shocking because God had just called Moses to go to Egypt. Moses was on his way to do what God asked him to do. Even though he did complain about it quite a bit before he set off. This brings up a couple of questions.

- Why was God going to kill him along the way when he was doing what God asked him to do?
- How did Zipporah know what to do to stop it?

There is speculation on both questions, but a definite answer is not found in scripture.

Some suggest God was angry with Moses because he was chosen to lead the Israelites and teach them the law, but he wasn't following the law himself. In Genesis 17:9–14, God commands circumcision.

> *Then God said to Abraham, "As for you, you must keep my covenant, you and your descendants after you for the generations to come. This is my covenant with you and your descendants after you, the covenant you are to keep: Every male among you shall be circumcised. You are to undergo circumcision, and it will be the sign of the covenant between me and you. For the generations to come every male among you who is eight days old must be circumcised, including those born in your household or bought with money from a foreigner—those who are not your offspring. Whether born in your household or bought with your money, they must be circumcised. My covenant in your flesh is to be an everlasting covenant. Any uncircumcised male, who has not been*

> *circumcised in the flesh, will be cut off from his people; he has broken my covenant. (Genesis 17:4–9)*

As for Zipporah, some suggest she may have been revolted by the practice. Maybe she didn't want Moses to circumcise their children on the eighth day as God commanded.

But when the attack came on Moses, she instinctively knew what the problem was and took action to save the life of her husband.

Three Lessons We Can Learn from Zipporah

1. Obey God even when we don't like it.

Obedience is serious.

Disobedience is what got us all into trouble in the first place back in the Garden of Eden.

We struggle doing what we're told and sometimes give into temptation. We're driven by our flesh instincts until we mature as Christians. Even then we still wrestle with them until we physically die.

Our obedience to God reflects our love for Him.

He's so gracious and merciful toward us. He gave His only Son to cover our sins as the perfect sacrifice. If we love Him, a desire to obey comes naturally out of thankfulness for His mercy toward us.

2. Do God's will (even if our spouse doesn't).

Scripture doesn't say whether she or Moses (or both) didn't want to circumcise their son—or, if they planned to but were delaying it for some reason. Delayed obedience is disobedience.

In scripture, we see she's the one who stepped in and intervened with obedience saving her husband's life. It may have been impossible for Moses to do anything at this point because God met with him and was about to kill him. Moses may have been physically incapacitated in the attack and unable to perform the circumcision.

Or was God *really* dealing with Zipporah? Maybe she was going along with Moses because they were married, but in her heart didn't want to obey God's commands. We don't know from scripture, but she did obey when God made it clear she must.

Doing God's will isn't just something we do when a tough decision comes along. It's living each day surrendered to His will and yielding to Him.

3. Recognize our own sin and repent.

In our own lives, when God brings some disobedience to our attention and makes it known to us, we should straighten it out right away. Do whatever needs to be done to make it right in His sight as soon as possible.

> *I will hasten and not delay to obey your commands.* (Psalm 119:60)

Like Moses, we may have been called by God into some specific ministry. Also, like Moses, we may have some sin in our lives we haven't dealt with yet.

God will likely bring the sin to our attention, so we recognize it and repent (or turn away from it). Then we can move forward in the good graces of God.

How We Can Apply These Lessons to Our Lives?

We are sinners. When we follow Jesus, we still sin even though we may be doing our best not to sin. It's in our blood. This is why the blood of Jesus Christ was required as the perfect sacrifice to cover our sins. Through Him, we are made right with God.

When we are moving along in our relationship with God through His Son, we will stumble along the way. It's a transformation process of becoming more like Jesus and saying goodbye to our old selves. We will do this naturally as Christians because of the indwelling Holy Spirit. He guides us, comforts us, and counsels us as we live our lives on earth.

When we disobey God's commands, the Holy Spirit begins making us aware of our sin. One way or another, He will bring it to our attention. Once we're aware, it's our job to correct it. Stop it. Make amends and do our best to never do it again.

This is a continual cycle in our spiritual life. Because we're so ingrained with sinfulness, once we learn the error of our ways about one sin, God begins to work on another area of our lives.

He's constantly ridding us of sin until we become more like His Son.

Recognizing sin in our lives and repenting are keys to growing up as a Christian. We want to be mature Christians and join God in His amazing work.

***This article was first published 7/23/2021 on Crosswalk.com

• CHAPTER 13 •

Four Lessons We Can Learn from Paul and Silas in Prison

I FOLLOW A FRIEND on social media who recently traveled to Greece. She and her husband went to many of the places Paul traveled. They visited the remains of the prison where Paul and Silas were imprisoned (Acts 16:22) and her posts intrigued me.

As I read her thoughts about traveling in Greece, her insights about Paul and Silas in prison resonated.

They were in prison and could have escaped but did not take advantage of the opportunity when it arose. They stayed where they were, and that decision ended up saving a man's life. Not only did it save his physical life, but he was saved spiritually along with his entire family.

What Is the Context of Paul and Silas in Prison?

Paul and Silas ended up in prison because they were being followed by a female slave possessed by a spirit. She earned money for her owners by fortune-telling. Even though she was stating truth regarding

Paul and Silas, and others with them, Paul was put out with her and cast the spirit from her in the name of Jesus Christ.

Her owners were angry because they lost their ability to make money using the female slave to predict the future.

They seized Paul and Silas and brought them before the authorities claiming they were Jews and advocating customs unlawful for Romans. Even though both Paul and Silas were both Roman citizens—they didn't argue and try to use a "get out of jail free" card.

They were stripped, beaten, and thrown into prison.

Four Lessons We Can Learn from Paul and Silas in Prison

1. They praised God while in prison.

Even though they'd been beaten and thrown in prison with their feet shackled, they sang hymns and prayed. Their praise in such a bad situation caused those around them to take notice and listen to them.

> *About midnight Paul and Silas were praying and singing hymns to God, and the other prisoners were listening to them. (Acts 16:25)*

2. Their praise not only helped them but also those who listened.

An earthquake shook the prison, and the doors flew open. **Everyone's** chains came loose.

> *Suddenly, there was such a violent earthquake that the foundations of the prison were shaken. At once all the prison doors flew open, and everyone's chains came loose. (Acts 16:26)*

3. What they *didn't* do was important.

Roman law required jailers to take personal responsibility for prisoners.

If Paul and Silas (and other prisoners) had bolted when their chains came loose, the jailer would have possibly been put to death. This is why he placed them into the inner prison and fastened their feet in stocks. By not escaping, they saved the life of the jailer.

> *The jailer woke up, and when he saw the prison doors open, he drew his sword and was about to kill himself because he thought the prisoners had escaped. But Paul shouted, "Don't harm yourself! We are all here!" (Acts 16:27–28)*

4. Their example changed lives eternally.

Paul and Silas chose to stay in the difficult circumstance they were in (prison) when they could have easily escaped suffering. That example drew the jailer to realize there was something different about them and he wanted whatever they had.

> *The jailer called for lights, rushed in and fell trembling before Paul and Silas. He then brought them out and asked, "Sirs, what must I do to be saved?" (Acts 16:29)*

In an incredible act of discernment, Paul knew they must not run when the chains came loose, and the prison doors swung open. He knew God was working and using the bad situation for something good.

The jailer was saved along with his family.

> They replied, "Believe in the Lord Jesus, and you will be saved—you and your household." Then they spoke the word of the Lord to him and to all the others in his house. At that hour of the night the jailer took them and washed their wounds; then immediately he and all his household were baptized. The jailer brought them into his house and set a meal before them; he was filled with joy because he had come to believe in God—he and his whole household. (Acts 16:31–34)

How to Apply These Lessons to Our Lives

There are many lessons to learn from Paul and Silas in prison and they're applicable to our Christian lives today.

It's all good.

When we're suffering in a bad situation, our instinct is to escape. We don't want to experience pain if we can get out of it.

But our praise to God in times of trouble is genuine. Because we're doing it *knowing* He's allowing the suffering for our good. Or the good of others.

It's easiest to praise God when we get the promotion, proposal, or a long-awaited fulfilled promise. It's much harder when we're suffering. Maybe we're in a situation where we don't see a good ending. We've lost someone we love. Or we're letting go of something we want to keep.

Raise the praise when trouble comes into our lives because **it's all good.**

> *And we know that in all things God works for the good of those who love him, who have been called according to his purpose. (Romans 8:28)*

Authentic worship is powerful.

Like a supernatural earthquake at just the right time, God moves powerfully in our lives when our worship is authentic. (No truer can it be than when we're in pain.) We trust Him with every part of our lives. The good and the bad.

When we surrender our suffering to Him—knowing it's part of His plan—we will find rest in **His** work.

God sets us free from our own prisons. He loosens our feet from shackles even when we're unaware we're bound. He heals what can only be healed by Him.

I trusted in the LORD when I said, "I am greatly afflicted." (Psalm 116:10)

What we *don't* do can be important.

Our flesh may desperately want to act, but when we stay still, we may impact someone else's life.

Christians are judged by the world. They look to see how we will act and what we'll do when we're in a bad situation. Will we bust out the door and head for the hills when times get tough? Or will we seek God and search for His purpose in the circumstances we find ourselves in?

What we don't do can be important to a lost person keeping tabs on Christian behavior. We all make mistakes and sin, but we need to remember we're called to a higher standard than the world and what we *don't do* is important.

A good example may change lives.

Paul and Silas set an incredible example of Christianity by staying in prison when they could have easily escaped their suffering.

Their behavior in prison affected other prisoners and the jailer.

Consider the example set by Paul and Silas in prison and remember our behavior may also affect other people. What another sees in us in times of trouble can have a deep impact. They may see how we handle a situation and use us as their example to follow.

My friend mentioned this quote from Joseph Campbell: "The cave you fear to enter holds the treasure you seek."

Paul didn't plan to go to prison yet he was willing to submit to God, continuing to praise Him even in shackles. His willingness to suffer and yet find joy in the moment is something we all can apply to our lives.

***This article was first published 11/19/2021 on Crosswalk.com

• CHAPTER 14 •

Is It Biblical to Pray for Our Pets?

To be honest, I never thought to pray for my pets.

Both our cat and dog have been healthy and I've never considered adding them to my prayer list.

Lincoln is the first dog I've truly loved deeply. I fell madly in love with him the moment I held him as a six-week-old puppy. He's so ood-natured and such a friendly dog. Our sassy black cat lives outside and catches lots of mice, moles, and (sadly) baby rabbits.

But as I pondered writing this article, I had a bad dream.

In the dream, my sweet dog, Lincoln, was having terrible stomach issues and I was afraid he was going to die. I could see blood about to spill from his body so I covered the first spot I saw with my left hand. Then I saw another spot pop up so I covered it with my other hand. I was in full panic mode at this point not knowing how I could call 911 for help because I was afraid if I moved my hands from him, he'd surely die. I woke up in a terrible state.

I rolled over with my heart aching for my pet. I worried he had some unknown health issue and I began to pray for him completely out of instinct.

After I prayed, I remembered how I'd never prayed for my pets that I could recall. Yet it came second nature when I grew concerned about a possible health issue.

If we believe in God then we know He made our sweet pets and gave them to us. We know He can do miraculous things when we seek Him and ask for help.

What Does the Bible Say about Caring for Animals?

Most scripture about animals in the Bible has to do with creation and animal sacrifice. God delights in His creation but does not delight in animal sacrifice. Even though it was required by law in the Old Testament to cover sin.

> *"The multitude of your sacrifices—what are they to me?" says the LORD. "I have more than enough of burnt offerings, of rams and the fat of fattened animals; I have no pleasure in the blood of bulls and lambs and goats."* (Isaiah 1:11)

Thank goodness Jesus came and fulfilled the law making a way for us to be right with God through His perfect sacrifice covering all of our sin. Through Him we are forgiven. No more animal sacrifice required. Jesus has us covered!

As with all creation, the animals God made are amazing! How they know exactly what to do is mind-blowing. His creation is perfection. He loves them and made them with great purpose. (Even though I'm going to ask about a couple of them I don't like much when I get to heaven.)

Of course, God loves our pets. He expects us to care for them and knows how much we love them. Because we've been created in God's image, we too want to care for animals and provide for their needs.

The lions roar for their prey and seek their food from God. (Psalm 104:21)

Is It Biblical to Pray for Our Pets?

Christians are advised to pray about **everything** in Philippians:

> *Do not be anxious about anything, but in every situation, by prayer and petition, with thanksgiving, present your requests to God. And the peace of God, which transcends all understanding, will guard your hearts and your minds in Christ Jesus. (Philippians 4:6–7)*

Of course, we should pray for our pets. We should pray for *anything* we care about.

When a pet is sick or lost, we become anxious because they're a great concern for us. We love them so much. They deserve to be included in our prayers. God cares about the smallest details of our lives. He certainly cares for the animals we care for and love.

A Prayer for a Lost Pet

I've never lost a beloved pet but my mom lost her dog a while back. He was let outside like he'd been many times before but he never came back to the door. They looked everywhere. She put ads in the local paper and family members posted on social media trying to find him.

Many months later, she still doesn't have her sweet Buddy back. Her heart is broken and she still hopes he will be brought back to her soon. The love she has for him shows in her voice when she speaks of him. She misses him terribly.

Not knowing what happened to a pet can be unsettling. Even though we may not know where they are or what happened to them, God does. We can ask for help in this situation and to be able to accept the outcome whatever it may be.

> *Heavenly Father,*
>
> *Thank you for giving us animals to care for and love.*
>
> *We ask for Your guidance to find our beloved pet. You know the depth of our love and how much we miss them. Please give us insight to the whereabouts of our pet. Show us where we might search to bring them home as soon as possible.*
>
> *If someone has found our pet, please move them to seek us out so we may get our pet back quickly.*
>
> *We know nothing is hidden from You. You know everything.*

If it's not possible for us to have them back then we thank You for allowing us to have our sweet pet for the time we've had them.

In the powerful name of Jesus Christ, Amen.

Your righteousness is like the highest mountains, your justice like the great deep. You, LORD, preserve both people and animals. (Psalm 36:6)

A Prayer for a Sick Pet

Dear Lord,

Thank you for giving us our sweet fur baby. We ask You to help him feel better as quickly as possible. Please help the vet figure out what is going on and advise us how to care for him properly to get him well.

Help us to do everything possible within our ability to help our pet get through this illness. They bring us such joy and unconditional love. We want the absolute best for them.

Give our pet a calmness as he goes through this illness and the ability to get through it with little bad affects. We pray this illness doesn't lead to the loss of life. We ask for complete healing and restoration for our pet.

In the powerful name of Jesus, Amen.

In His hand is the life of every creature and the breath of all mankind. (Job 12:10)

A Prayer for a Dying Pet

There may come a time when we have to say goodbye. It might break our hearts.

So many have had to make the agonizing decision to put their pet down due to health issues. I can't imagine because I haven't been in this situation. But my love for Lincoln is so deep the thought of saying goodbye to him is heartbreaking.

> *Heavenly Father,*
>
> *Thank you for the life you've given our sweet pet. We praise You for allowing us to share so many good times together. He's brought more joy to our family than we could have ever imagined. He holds a very special place in our hearts.*
>
> *He is family.*
>
> *We don't want to say goodbye. It hurts knowing we'll never see or hold him again. The emptiness will be difficult. Our world will never be the same without him.*
>
> *Help us to get through this loss. Give us comfort knowing we were allowed to have him for the time we did. We love him deeply. We will never forget the love and joy he brought to our lives.*
>
> *In the mighty name of Jesus Christ, we pray. Amen.*

Are not five sparrows sold for two pennies? Yet not one of them is forgotten by God. (Luke 12:6)

How Praying for Pets Can Bring Comfort

Praying for our pets brings comfort because we trust God. We know His way is best for us and for our pets.

We trust their health, well-being, and everyday life in the hands of God. He created them and loves them more than we will ever understand or know until we get to heaven.

Pray along with them for pets, for vets, and for those who care for abused or neglected animals.

> *The righteous care for the needs of their animals, but the kindest acts of the wicked are cruel. (Proverbs 12:10)*

***This article was first published 5/11/2021 on Crosswalk.com

• CHAPTER 15 •

Is It Possible to Give Too Much?

MOST PEOPLE WOULD AGREE giving is a *good* thing.

Some of us are better at it than others though. In our efforts to be generous and give, we sometimes give the wrong things or too much.

When I was a kid, sometimes I'd spend my birthday money on my siblings. I enjoyed being able to share but I'd end up with nothing for my birthday (except the short-lived good feeling I got from giving to others). Then days later, when I had nothing to show for the money I received, I'd question my decision to give it all away.

Later in life, I realized my gift-giving skills needed major work. Instead of taking the time to think of what a person may like as a gift, I'd buy them something I liked hoping they'd like it too.

Once, I bought my future mother-in-law a framed piece of art for Christmas. She had a lot of ceramic cats in her house. But did I buy her an artwork of a beautiful cat?

Nope. It was a picture of a chicken. Bless her heart. She hung it on her kitchen wall, and it stayed there for years. Later on, when I learned to buy better presents, I mentioned to her it wouldn't hurt my feelings if she took it down. (Which she did by the next time I visited.)

It took me a long time to figure out how to give good gifts. Either I gave away things and later regretted it or I'd give someone a gift, but it wasn't what they'd like at all.

Is It Possible to Give Too Much?

Absolutely.

Giving wrong gifts is one thing but giving too much can be a big problem if we don't know when to stop or set some boundaries.

We may put so much of ourselves into our marriage and family life we end up losing ourselves and feeling lost. We can give our time and talents so much doing church activities, we get completely burned out.

Maybe there are underlying issues, and we have *unrecognized* selfish motives for giving so much.

> *All a person's ways seem pure to them, but motives are weighed by the LORD.* (Proverbs 16:2)

Here are four reasons we may give too much.

1. We can't say no.

Sometimes saying no is the right thing to do. Even if it feels selfish. Setting boundaries and priorities are important for a healthy life. It's okay to say no to some things and yes to other things. Seek God in your choices and serve Him in everything you choose.

> *Whatever you do, work at it with all your heart, as working for the Lord, not for human masters. (Colossians 3:23)*

2. We want others to know we give.

Once, I witnessed a pastor open an envelope addressed to him from a church member. Inside was the member's cash offering. Instead of putting the money in the offering plate, they addressed an envelope directly to him.

A little odd but maybe they had a reason for giving in such a way. However, it appeared as if they wanted to make sure he knew what they'd given.

> *"Be careful not to practice your righteousness in front of others to be seen by them. If you do, you will have no reward from your Father in heaven. So when you give to the needy, do not announce it with trumpets, as the hypocrites do in the synagogues and on the streets, to be honored by others. Truly I tell you, they have received their reward in full. But when you give to the needy, do not let your left hand know what your right hand is doing, so that your giving may be in secret. Then your Father, who sees what is done in secret, will reward you. (Matthew 6:1–4)*

3. We're compelled by a sense of duty.

We can feel so dedicated to family or church activities that we do, do, do until we drop. Whether we're giving of ourselves or giving financially, we shouldn't give out of compulsion but from our hearts.

> *Each of you should give what you have decided in your heart to give, not reluctantly or under compulsion, for God loves a cheerful giver. (2 Corinthians 9:7)*

4. We are people pleasers.

No matter how much we give or how nice we are, there will be people who don't care for us. It doesn't matter what we do. To a people pleaser, it can be hard to find out another person doesn't like us.

Do we seek approval from people when we should be seeking it from God?

> *Yet at the same time many even among the leaders believed in him. But because of the Pharisees they would not openly acknowledge their faith for fear they would be put out of the synagogue; for they loved human praise more than praise from God. (John 12:42–43)*

It was easy for me to come up with these reasons because I've struggled with each one. Sometimes, I'm too nice and don't want to say no. Sometimes I want people to like me, and I'm compelled by a sense of duty. I used to be a people pleaser but no more.

The Bible contains a variation of the word *give* 1,433 times. That's a lot! It shows just how much God cares about giving.

He gave the greatest gift of all. But He also had boundaries. Yes, the gift of salvation is for all, but only through Jesus. He gave the perfect, required sacrifice we're incapable of giving.

Jesus is the gift. He's also the boundary.

The best way to give is to give like God does.

He says no sometimes.

> *When you ask, you do not receive, because you ask with wrong motives, that you may spend what you get on your pleasures. (James 4:3)*

He never gives the wrong thing.

> *Every good and perfect gift is from above, coming down from the Father of the heavenly lights, who does not change like shifting shadows. (James 1:17)*

He gives us what we need.

> *And my God will meet all your needs according to the riches of his glory in Christ Jesus. (Philippians 4:19)*

He knows how to give us good gifts.

> *If you, then, though you are evil, know how to give good gifts to your children, how much more will your Father in heaven give good gifts to those who ask him! (Matthew 7:11)*

We can give too much of a lot of things, but we can never give too much of Jesus.

The world is desperate for Him. They just don't know it. When people are hurting, we can give them Jesus in some way. Whether it's a gentle hug or a word of encouragement given at just the right time. We share Him by showing love to others. We may even be given the chance to tell them about our wonderful Savior and they may decide to follow Jesus.

What an honor and a privilege it is for Christians to give Jesus to the world. God gave us this perfect gift to be given to others. A gift like no other and desperately needed.

> *"A new command I give you: Love one another. As I have loved you, so you must love one another. (John 13:34)*

***This article was first published 2/16/2022 on Crosswalk.com

• CHAPTER 16 •

Three Lessons We Can Learn from Noah's Drunkenness

MOST CHRISTIANS ARE QUITE familiar with the story of Noah's ark. How God sent a great flood and destroyed all life on earth except for those sheltered within the ark with Noah and his family.

After they survive the flood and find land, God makes a covenant with Noah and promises never to flood the entire earth again. He gives the rainbow as a sign of the covenant.

> *And God said, "This is the sign of the covenant I am making between me and you and every living creature with you, a covenant for all generations to come: I have set my rainbow in the clouds, and it will be the sign of the covenant between me and the earth. Whenever I bring clouds over the earth and the rainbow appears in the clouds, I will remember my covenant between me and you and all living creatures of every kind. Never again will the waters become a flood to destroy all life. Whenever the rainbow appears in the clouds, I will see it and remember the everlasting covenant between*

> *God and all living creatures of every kind on the earth." So, God said to Noah, "This is the sign of the covenant I have established between me and all life on the earth." (Genesis 9:12–17)*

Some may not be as familiar with what happened next: the incident with Noah's drunkenness and how it affected his family. A curse came for Canaan after the covenant.

What Does the Bible Tell Us about the drunkenness of Noah?

Noah had planted a vineyard and became drunk after drinking some wine. He was inside his tent, passed out and naked. His youngest son, Ham, saw him naked and told his two brothers.

> *Noah, a man of the soil, proceeded to plant a vineyard. When he drank some of its wine, he became drunk and lay uncovered inside his tent. Ham, the father of Canaan, saw his father naked and told his two brothers outside. But Shem and Japheth took a garment and laid it across their shoulders; then they walked in backward and covered their father's naked body. Their faces were turned the other way so that they would not see their father naked. (Genesis 9:20–23)*

There is debate among scholars about what happened between Ham and Noah. Some believe something serious may have happened and Ham may have violated his father in some way. But this is only speculation. Obviously, Ham dishonored his father by seeing him naked and by telling his brothers. Some believe he may have mocked Noah.

We see Shem and Japheth showing respect to Noah by covering his nakedness and walking backward to avoid seeing him in such a vulnerable state.

Interestingly, feeling shame because of nakedness in the Garden of Eden was a consequence of the original sin of mankind. Then there is the first animal sacrifice as God made clothing for them and covered them.

> *The LORD God made garments of skin for Adam and his wife and covered them. (Genesis 3:21)*

Similarly, we see Noah's two sons covering their father's nakedness.

Three Lessons We Can Learn from the Drunkenness of Noah

1. At what point does drinking alcohol become a sin?

Having a drink containing alcohol is not a sin.

The word *wine* is found in the Bible over 200 times in good ways and bad ways. Wine was used in drink offerings in the Temple. It's mentioned being used at times of celebration. Jesus turned water into wine (really good wine) at a wedding celebration.

Paul advises Timothy to drink a little wine for his health.

> *Stop drinking only water, and use a little wine because of your stomach and your frequent illnesses. (1 Timothy 5:23)*

Its overuse is the problem because it causes drunkenness and addiction. Drinking alcohol to the point of drunkenness is when it becomes a sin.

> *Listen, my son, and be wise, and set your heart on the right path: Do not join those who drink too much wine or gorge themselves on meat, for drunkards and gluttons become poor, and drowsiness clothes them in rags. (Proverbs 23:19–21)*

2. What makes drunkenness a sin?

The word *drunk* is found in scripture over sixty times. Most relate to drunkenness and show it as something to avoid.

Self-control is one of the fruits of the Spirit evident in believers. The loss of self-control is what makes drunkenness a sin.

> *But the fruit of the Spirit is love, joy, peace, forbearance, kindness, goodness, faithfulness, gentleness, and self-control. Against such things there is no law. (Galatians 5:22–23)*

When our guard is down because of alcohol consumption, we may make bad decisions. We may find ourselves in bad situations we never would have gotten ourselves into if we were sober.

> *Do not get drunk on wine, which leads to debauchery. Instead, be filled with the Spirit, (Ephesians 5:18)*

For those (like me) who may not know the definition of *debauchery*, it is defined as excessive indulgence in sensual pleasures. This verse alone in Ephesians is enough warning about what can happen when we drink too much alcohol.

3. What are the consequences of Noah's drunkenness?

There were generational consequences for the incident with Noah's drunkenness.

Even though Ham sinned, it was his son, Canaan, who was cursed.

> *When Noah awoke from his wine and found out what his youngest son had done to him, he said, "Cursed be Canaan! The lowest of slaves will he be to his brothers." He also said, "Praise be to the LORD, the God of Shem! May Canaan be the slave of Shem. May God extend Japheth's territory; may Japheth live in the tents of Shem and may Canaan be the slave of Japheth." (Genesis 9:24–27)*

One interesting consequence is the Canaanites were driven out of the Promised Land when the Israelites took possession of it after wandering in the desert for forty years.

These days, there are consequences for anyone who finds themselves in a state of drunkenness. With no self-control, we may sit behind the wheel of a car and drive, which can lead to our own death or the death of an innocent person. This would be a dreadful, lifelong consequence. Some will become addicted with just one sip, and it can cause numerous issues in life.

> *Wine is a mocker and beer a brawler; whoever is led astray by them is not wise. (Proverbs 20:1)*

Even though we're all sinners, through the power of the Holy Spirit, God is making us more like Jesus. He brings to our attention sin that needs repentance. When we're convicted about a particular sin, we should turn from it and do our best not to give in to the temptation to sin in that way again. Then God will move onto our next sin issue whether it's known to us or not. He may need to make us aware, so we can turn away from it bringing Him the glory.

As Christians, we should strive to bring glory to God in every place in our lives.

> *So whether you eat or drink or whatever you do, do it all for the glory of God. (1 Corinthians 10:31)*

****This article was first published 12/15/2021 on Crosswalk.com*

· CHAPTER 17 ·

How to Keep Your Sanity When Caring for a Loved One with Alzheimer's

ALZHEIMER'S IS A THIEF.

It slowly takes a loved one into a confused, dark place and steals the person we love—robbing the family blind.

My beloved dad passed away in September 2019 due to this terrible disease. Mom kept him home longer than she should have because she couldn't bear to put him into a nursing home. She was only able to manage because some of my sisters and brothers lived nearby and were on call 24/7. One sister took the brunt of it because Dad thought she was his wife. She had the ability to calm him down when sundowners set in and he was acting out in his confusion.

Mom finally gave in about the nursing home and he spent his last few weeks there. Once that happened, he went downhill quickly. He was brought back home and passed away the same day within an hour of arriving home in the ambulance. He relaxed when he was back in the house he built and in the presence of his family again and breathed his last breath.

The man who preached in so many little churches about God's grace and mercy was finally with his beloved Savior. It was a *long* road home. The grieving came slowly but surely over time as he declined. Countless tears shed over many years before he finally passed away. We were relieved for him because he was finished suffering yet devastated not to have him with us anymore.

One thing Dad never forgot were hymns. He sang stanza after stanza that I couldn't remember the words to but they were ingrained into his mind from years of singing them. I can only imagine the praise songs he's been singing since he got to heaven.

When one is suffering with Alzheimer's, the journey home can be long. Being a caregiver for a loved one with this terrible disease can be frustrating, stressful, and full of heartache.

Here are some simple ways to keep your sanity when caring for a loved one with Alzheimer's.

1. Use music.

Hymns are rooted deep in the hearts of many older Christians. The familiar melodies take the listener back to a comforting place. When I hear most hymns, I'm back in the little church I grew up in, singing alto with the congregation.

Sing hymns.

Play a soothing instrument such as a guitar.

Sing popular songs from their younger years.

Play a CD of gentle nature sounds such as ocean waves.

2. Meet them where they are and *go with it.*

It can be confusing when we're in the present and they talk about someone who passed away many years earlier as if they are in the other room. But if that's where they are at that moment then go with it.

If they're insistent that they want to visit someone they think is alive but they're already dead, take them for a drive and *pretend* for a little while that you're going to see them. They will eventually forget about it and you can take them back home.

If you take them to the graveyard and explain to them that their loved one is dead, they will relive the death over and over again.

3. Don't correct them or argue with them.

There's no point in correcting someone who will forget what they said in about one minute. It will frustrate the caregiver and stress out the one suffering with Alzheimer's. They truly can't help it.

Play along with what they say or distract them. Try to get them interested in something else such as browsing through a photo album.

You can have one created just for them with photos of their parents, siblings, children, and grandchildren.

4. Get some rest!

Caregiving for a loved one with Alzheimer's is exhausting. Dad was always trying to go home so he took off many times. It's dangerous and scary when they slip off undetected and a search party has to be called in.

Again, it's the family living nearby taking the brunt of this. Though living far away from the loved one is also stressful because not being there to help when you'd like to is painful, too, and you feel anxious about leaving the load on the shoulders of others in the family.

- Take weekend shifts to give others a break.
- When you're off for a weekend, get away and relax.
- Hire a professional caregiver, if possible.
- Hire a housekeeper (one less thing!).

5. Try a few helpful tips for dealing with late-day confusion or "sundowners."

- Limit daytime naps (difficult to do when the caregiver is exhausted).
- Limit caffeine and sugar.
- Keep a daytime routine and try to create a routine for evenings and bedtime.
- Limit television viewing in the evenings.

6. Practice love, grace, and patience.

There's no substitute for love. The fact that you're caring for someone with Alzheimer's shows just how much you love them.

They may need to be touched. If so, offer a hug. Dad liked to get his back scratched and that's what I did the last time I visited him in the nursing home.

Extend grace to the patient and other caregivers. It's okay to laugh sometimes at the crazy situations that arise when going through this journey. Sometimes, laughter is the best medicine to help manage the madness.

Through experience, I know all of this is easier said than done.

Truly, seeing a loved one go through the stages of this disease is dreadful. How many times do we just want a conversation like we used to have but it's no longer possible? We might get a glimpse of the person we once knew but it's rare when they have declined into the later stages.

After Dad's funeral, I browsed through old photos of him on my laptop. How wonderful it is to see his smiling face and eyes sparkling with life, years before he began to forget.

> What I'd give to have him back the way he used to be before Alzheimer's riddled his mind and body!

As I contemplated my earthly father and how much I'd give to have him back the way he used to be, another thought crossed my mind.

> What would God give to have us back the way we were before we were racked with sin and fallen?

EVERYTHING.

He gave His only Son to get us back.

> For God so loved the world that he gave his one and only Son, that whoever believes in him shall not perish but have eternal life. (John 3:16)

Never forget we are deeply loved by our heavenly Father who gave **everything** to have us back. Through His Son, we are made new.

Diseases may steal our loved ones but God gives new life.

Trust Him with everything.

***This article was first published 8/7/2020 on Crosswalk.com

• CHAPTER 18 •

Five Truths We Can Take Away from King Solomon's Story

THE KING SOLOMON STORY is intriguing. While born in times of war, he reigned in times of peace. He's the second son of King David and Bathsheba.

Solomon is supposed to be the next king, but he has a brother, Adonijah, who steps up and takes the throne without King David or God's blessing. Of course, this is short-lived, and Solomon becomes king.

He's well known for his God-given wisdom, wealth, and power. He reigned as king of Israel for forty years and built the magnificent Temple in Jerusalem just like God said. (1 Chronicles 28:5) He wrote the book of Proverbs and the Song of Solomon in the Bible.

He had an astounding 700 wives and 300 concubines. Some of those wives turned his heart after false gods and led him into idolatry.

The King Solomon story has many truths for us to glean for our lives as Christians.

Here are five truths from the King Solomon story.

1. Being uninvited may be an invitation to see God work.

When King David was on his deathbed, his son Adonijah decided he'd be the next king.

> *Now Adonijah, whose mother was Haggith, put himself forward and said, "I will be king." So he got chariots and horses ready, with fifty men to run ahead of him. (His father had never rebuked him by asking, "Why do you behave as you do?" He was also very handsome and was born next after Absalom.)*
>
> *Adonijah conferred with Joab son of Zeruiah and with Abiathar the priest, and they gave him their support. But Zadok the priest, Benaiah son of Jehoiada, Nathan the prophet, Shimei and Rei, and David's special guard did not join Adonijah.*
>
> *Adonijah then sacrificed sheep, cattle, and fattened calves at the Stone of Zoheleth near En Rogel. He invited all his brothers, the king's sons, and all the royal officials of Judah, but* **he did not invite** *Nathan the prophet or Benaiah or the special guard or his brother Solomon. (1 Kings 1:5–9)*

Solomon was not invited to the party along with a few others. However, it was an opportunity to see God work on his behalf. When word got back to King David that the wrong son had stepped into his position, he made things right and blessed Solomon officially making him the next king.

It can be painful when we're not included when we hope to be invited. We should look at it as an opportunity instead of rejection. If God wanted us there, we would have been invited.

2. Something coming to us from God is legit.

> "As you know," he said, "the kingdom was mine. All Israel looked to me as their king. But things changed, and the kingdom has gone to my brother; for it has come to him from the LORD. (1 Kings 2:15)

Solomon was *supposed* to be king not Adonijah. I love how this verse states: "It has come to him from the LORD."

If something comes to us from God, it can't be stopped. If what we're seeking falls apart then we need to let it go. God has something better (and it will be legit).

3. God may give *more* than we request.

In a dream, God asks Solomon to ask for anything he wants, and then gave him *more* than he requested.

> At Gibeon the LORD appeared to Solomon during the night in a dream, and God said, "Ask for whatever you want me to give you."

Solomon answered, "You have shown great kindness to your servant, my father David, because he was faithful to you and righteous and upright in heart. You have continued this great kindness to him and have given him a son to sit on his throne this very day.

"Now, LORD my God, you have made your servant king in place of my father David. But I am only a little child and do not know how to carry out my duties. Your servant is here among the people you have chosen, a great people, too numerous to count or number. So give your servant a discerning heart to govern your people and to distinguish between right and wrong. For who is able to govern this great people of yours?"

The Lord was pleased that Solomon had asked for this. So God said to him, "Since you have asked for this and not for long life or wealth for yourself, nor have asked for the death of your enemies but for discernment in administering justice, I will do what you have asked. I will give you a wise and discerning heart, so that there will never have been anyone like you, nor will there ever be. Moreover, I will give you what you have not asked for—both wealth and honor—so that in your lifetime you will have no equal among kings. And if you walk in obedience to me and keep my decrees and commands as David your father did, I will give you a long life." Then Solomon awoke—and he realized it had been a dream. (1 Kings 3:5–15)

When we make a request in prayer *believing* God will answer with a humble heart, He may deliver more than we expect or ask.

God sees the heart and knows our intentions. If He likes what He sees, like the perfect parent He is, He may give us what we've asked for but also bless us beyond our expectations.

4. Our relationship with God affects unbelievers.

The Queen of Sheba heard about the fame of Solomon and his relationship to God, so she wanted to test him with hard questions. It didn't take her long to see Solomon was even wiser than she'd heard, and nothing was too hard for him.

> *She said to the king, "The report I heard in my own country about your achievements and your wisdom is true. But I did not believe these things until I came and saw with my own eyes. Indeed, not even half was told me; in wisdom and wealth you have far exceeded the report I heard. How happy your people must be! How happy your officials, who continually stand before you and hear your wisdom! Praise be to the LORD your God, who has delighted in you and placed you on the throne of Israel. Because of the LORD's eternal love for Israel, he has made you king to maintain justice and righteousness." (1 Kings 10:6–9)*

It's interesting that she comes to meet Solomon with an attitude of unbelief and skepticism but leaves with praise on her lips for the Living God.

We can have this same effect on others at times when they see our genuine relationship with God and how He works in our lives. Sharing our testimony with coworkers or neighbors can impact their lives and lead unsaved people to seek a relationship with God.eHe

5. Others may turn *our* hearts from God.

> *King Solomon, however, loved many foreign women besides Pharaoh's daughter—Moabites, Ammonites, Edomites, Sidonians, and Hittites. They were from nations about which the LORD had told the Israelites, "You must not intermarry with them, because they will surely turn your hearts after their gods." Nevertheless, Solomon held fast to them in love. He had seven hundred wives of royal birth and three hundred concubines, and his wives led him astray. As Solomon grew old, his wives turned his heart after other gods, and his heart was not fully devoted to the LORD his God, as the heart of David his father had been. He followed Ashtoreth the goddess of the Sidonians, and Molek the detestable god of the Ammonites. So Solomon did evil in the eyes of the LORD; he did not follow the LORD completely, as David his father had done.*

> *On a hill east of Jerusalem, Solomon built a high place for Chemosh the detestable god of Moab, and for Molek the detestable god of the Ammonites. He did the same for all his foreign wives, who burned incense and offered sacrifices to their gods. The LORD became angry with Solomon because*

his heart had turned away from the LORD, the God of Israel, who had appeared to him twice. (1 Kings 11:1–9)

Christians are called to love deeply. But there's a fine line between loving someone (or something) deeply and loving someone (or something) *more* than we love God. We may not even realize we're loving *or trusting* in an inappropriate way.

Anything in life we worship in some way other than God is idolatry. In the day of Solomon, they literally worshiped other gods. Today, even Christians worship other gods. Often, we don't mean to but many things in our lives can become an idol.

This can be a town we love, a job, a spouse, money, and even our beliefs if we don't allow the Holy Spirit to correct us and guide us along the path in life God has for us.

God will tear down the idols in a Christian's life. He may allow job loss, financial struggles, and hidden sins brought to light. Whatever is standing between Him and our whole hearts in worship must be put in its proper place.

God wants our whole hearts in obedience, devotion, and love.

***This article was first published 9/2/2021 on Crosswalk.com

• CHAPTER 19 •

How to Let Go of Family Traditions and Embrace New Ones

Nobody prepared me for letting go of family traditions. To be honest, I really never thought that far ahead of my daily life raising a family.

But sooner *than* later, my first two sons were no longer little boys but had grown into men. My little family grew larger through marriage and we were blessed with two daughters-in-law.

The blessings are innumerable. Nothing compares to the added deep love the little grands bring when they're born. Such sweet gifts from God. Truly, the cherry on top of the dessert of life.

With those wonderful family additions came other changes I never considered as my children grew up. Our family traditions changed.

It wasn't just about our little family of five anymore. It became about the families of spouses and managing to work holiday celebrations around everyone else's family schedules.

I was disheartened at first. It seemed my life changed so quickly and letting go of family traditions was more difficult than I imagined it would be. In the blink of an eye, it seemed, my little Christmas morning family celebrations were over.

Before I knew it, we were left celebrating with the lone teenager left in the house on Christmas morning watching him open gifts. He felt a little awkward and we realized we needed to make a change.

So, the next Christmas, we opened all of our gifts on Christmas Eve with the whole family together instead of having a separate Christmas morning celebration with what's left of the family at home. That way, we could all sleep in, which is what teenagers love anyway.

It must happen as we grow older and move along the path of life. But a lot of things are harder than I thought they'd be now that I'm crossing that bridge I finally came to.

It hurts to put in the past the things we want to keep in the present.

Through this season of life, I managed to learn a few things.

Here are some tips on how to let go of family traditions and embrace new ones.

1. Go with the flow.

When the kids get married and move away, there are other family traditions to consider. We may discover the actual day of the holiday is no longer available for our get-together. While this can disappoint us because we've always celebrated on the actual day, we must be flexible and give and take with our new family members.

This is hard to do, I know. It might also be frustrating. Especially, if we begin to feel our celebration is taking a backseat to everyone else's in the family.

But we need to remember young families are beginning their own celebrations as a family. We did the same thing when we started our own family. We honor the next generation by going with the flow when it comes to family gatherings.

Eventually, we will get together—whether it's sooner or later. Enjoy the time together and make the best of the situation.

These times are *memories* in the making.

> *See, I am doing a new thing! Now it springs up; do you not perceive it? I am making a way in the wilderness and streams in the wasteland. (Isaiah 43:19)*

2. Let go of expectations.

Some of our biggest disappointments in life come when we have unmet expectations. It's like we sabotage our own life. We expect certain things and when we don't get them; we become disappointed.

When we've been accustomed to celebrating a holiday a certain way and we're unable to do it any longer, we can become disappointed.

But we need to understand life will change year to year as we grow older and our traditions may also change.

They can actually become **better** if we're willing to adjust a bit.

I'll admit I was disappointed when we were unable to have an Easter egg hunt at the time I expected a couple of years ago. We ended up not being able to do it until it was dark outside. Needless to say, I had unmet expectations followed by disappointment.

However, we managed to have the Easter egg hunt in the dark using flashlights. Strange as it seems, it was one of the most fun times we've had as a family. (They even make glow-in-the dark eggs for just such an occasion these days.)

If we can manage to go with the flow and stay positive about schedules and expectations, we may discover new traditions born out of our need to make things work and they might be more fun and memorable.

> *For the LORD is good and his love endures forever; his faithfulness continues through all generations. (Psalm 100:5)*

3. Make new memories.

Since we can't stop change from taking place because it *is* the order of things, we may consider making new traditions for the family. Once we accept the changes taking place within our family, we can move forward creating lasting memories for our children and grandchildren.

If you remember a special tradition from a grandparent and loved it, recycle it and pass it on, down to the next generation.

My mother-in-law always had a scavenger hunt for the grandchildren with little notes hidden in different places in the house. Our kids loved trying to find the prize. When our grandchildren get a bit older, we will absolutely recycle this tradition.

But if not, create some new ones. If you're tech-savvy, check out the Internet for ideas because it's loaded. There are wonderful ideas for making crafts or interesting games to play when the family gets together.

As life goes by, we may not have any plans for the actual holiday or even the week of the holiday. It's time to consider new, satisfying traditions for *ourselves*. We can now do things we've always wanted to do but never seemed to have the time.

Here are a few ideas for making the most of those holidays when we get older and life changes.

Consider spending the holidays serving others at a homeless shelter or a local church serving meals to the less fortunate.

Make a meal or dessert for someone in your neighborhood or for a friend or relative you know is going through a rough time in life.

Intentionally seek God asking Him to reveal a need you can meet for another person.

Plan a short vacation and enjoy your time together with your spouse or a friend!

The most important tradition we *need* is to make sure we handle life changes well and honor God.

Our reaction to the ebb and flow of life as we age is in full view of the next generation. How we *lived* is an example for those family members coming after us. They may not understand any of it until *they* get older, but then they will see how God was **reflected** in our life.

Hopefully, they will seek the One who changed our lives and helped us get through our difficult days and blessed us with a **beautiful** life.

> *Tell it to your children, and let your children tell it to their children, and their children to the next generation. (Joel 1:3)*

***This article was first published 3/31/2021 on Crosswalk.com

• CHAPTER 20 •

How Do I Explain to Seekers Why My Church Asks for Money?

IT CAN BE HARD to explain to seekers why churches ask for money. It can also be unsettling to attend a new church and the first sermon you hear is about tithing. You can't help but think, *they're only after money.*

The first time I was informed I should give money to my church, I was taken aback. *Money?* Why do I need to give *my* money to the church? I was a teenager, spiritually immature, and spent my small paychecks on fuel for my car and fast food.

But we all need money and churches are no exception.

I never truly understood how much they need it until I was on the staff of a couple of churches as the Financial Secretary. I discovered many things about how tithes and offerings are used. The truth is, churches have bills. Some have very big bills. But that's not the most important reason we give.

Here are four simple thoughts on giving to help seekers understand why Christians give money to the church.

1. God is a giver.

We give because God made us in His image and He's a great **big giver**. He gave His one and only Son, Jesus, to redeem us because of His deep love.

We give back to God because of our deep love for **Him** and His work.

> *For God so loved the world that he gave his one and only Son, that whoever believes in him shall not perish but have eternal life. (John 3:16)*

2. Giving is an act of worship.

We sing praises, study, obey God's Word, and serve others to worship God in all of His goodness. But it's also worshipping God to give. Giving is having faith in Him and an act of *trust*.

We give back to God what is ***already*** His.

With our offering/tithe, we're saying to God,

> *"Thank you for giving me some finances to manage. I trust You with this offering to do what's best with it through my*

> local church. I know You will provide for my needs so I'm letting go of this money and giving it back to You."

There's a book to be written on how many years it took me to discover money wasn't mine. It can also take young Christians a long time to become consistent givers, let alone, tithers. But everything belongs to God. Including money.

> For in him all things were created: things in heaven and on earth, visible and invisible, whether thrones or powers or rulers or authorities; all things have been created through him and for him. (Colossians 1:16)

3. Christians support God's work through giving.

God's work is way bigger than we can imagine. How awesome it is that He invites us to be a part of it! It's so much more than church services on Sunday morning for members and visitors.

However, church finances do cover many different types of ministry such as Sunday school classes, Vacation Bible School, church camps for kids, etc.

Then there are bills. The electric bill alone can be many thousands of dollars if the building is large. Then, just like our homes, there's water, sewer, and phone bills. All cost a lot of money the larger the church is. But they also supply basic items needed for church services and fellowship gatherings like paper products such as toilet paper, paper towels, paper plates, cups, and napkins. They often provide coffee, creamer, sugar, tea, etc.

Some churches have a mortgage. Others may have purchased land, planning to build a new church and have a payment due monthly to cover that expense.

Most churches have paid staff. They have weekly or biweekly payroll coming out of the offering each week. Depending on how many people the church has on staff, the payroll can take up a large portion of the offering.

Even though they are tax exempt on purchases by being a 501(c)(3), a non-profit tax exempt charitable organization, they are responsible for payroll taxes, Social Security, and Medicare. They also may pay benefits such as vacation, sick time, and retirement plans.

4. Churches give, too!

Most churches give to charitable organizations and support other ministries in some financial way. Your offering/tithe not only supports the church you're giving to but also may help *many others* you're unaware of.

They may support a local ministry such as an unplanned pregnancy center to help women find support for their pregnancy instead of choosing abortion. They may support a ministry that supplies food and/or clothing to those in need. They may have a line in their budget for benevolence. Those funds would be given to folks in need as they arise throughout the year.

It's amazing what a financial gift can do when placed into the offering plate or given online to a local church.

Scriptures about Giving

> *One person gives freely, yet gains even more; another withholds unduly, but comes to poverty. (Proverbs 11:24)*

> *Each of you should give what you have decided in your heart to give, not reluctantly or under compulsion, for God loves a cheerful giver. (2 Corinthians 9:7)*

> *"Do not store up for yourselves treasures on earth, where moths and vermin destroy, and where thieves break in and steal. But store up for yourselves treasures in heaven, where moths and vermin do not destroy, and where thieves do not break in and steal. (Matthew 6:19–20)*

> *For where your treasure is, there your heart will be also. (Matthew 6:21)*

> *As Jesus looked up, he saw the rich putting their gifts into the temple treasury. He also saw a poor widow put in two very small copper coins. "Truly I tell you," he said, "this poor widow has put in more than all the others. All these people gave their gifts out of their wealth; but she out of her poverty put in all she had to live on." (Luke 21:1–4)*

Sometimes, in life, we might find ourselves unable to give the way we'd like to due to hardships such as job loss, medical problems, etc. Maybe we're in a financial situation where if we tithe, we can't pay our bills. This is not good but it happens from time to time in life. In this situation, we should give what we can. It may be much less than we'd like to give but the attitude of our heart is more important than any amount of money we place in the offering plate. God loves a *cheerful giver,* and He knows what we're going through.

We're all growing closer to God *individually* and giving is part of the growing process. The Holy Spirit is working to make us into the person God wants us to be. This is a slow growth process and can take time. What a person gives financially to a church is completely between **the giver and God.**

He is so good to His children. Giving back will eventually become a strong desire of the seeker's heart.

> *What shall I return to the LORD for all his goodness to me? I will lift up the cup of salvation and call on the name of the LORD. I will fulfill my vows to the LORD in the presence of all his people.* (Psalm 116:12–14)

***This article was first published 6/10/2020 on Crosswalk.com

• CHAPTER 21 •

Three Ways We Can Guard Our Hearts

A HEART IS PRECIOUS to God.

Most are easy to love but also easily broken. If we're not careful, our tender hearts can become hardened by life. They may become bitter and even numb. Neither of those are good.

Bitterness creeps in from continuous disappointments or unmet expectations. But numbness is most often due to pain. It's self-protection. We may not even realize we've lost all feeling.

A numb heart is really a hard heart. It just got that way through pain, and we didn't intend for it to happen. But it can be healed and once again, become tender.

In scripture, the word *heart* is mentioned 725 times. Most are found in Psalms. David poured out his heart when he wrote about God. I'm so thankful he did because it's my favorite place to find solace in God's Word.

There are many descriptive words for heart issues in Psalms: *contrite, proud, anguished, cunning, callused, grieved, blameless, disloyal,* and *unfaithful*. These are just a few but we can see from these varying types of hearts how it should be guarded.

But what exactly does that mean?

Our first instinct might be to put walls up around our heart to protect it. We think this is guarding. But it's not protecting the way God intends. Eventually, we may discover the numbness has set in. Through our efforts to guard our heart—we've closed it off instead.

Building walls will not protect us. Seeking God is the only true protection. But guarding our hearts is complicated because our nature wants to keep pain away. However, God often uses pain to teach us and to draw us into a closer relationship with Him.

> *Above all else, guard your heart, for everything you do flows from it. (Proverbs 4:23)*

I listened to a Christian counselor recently discuss this verse. Her words brought to my attention how important it is to us as we go through our lives. The first three words in this verse are quite striking. We should guard our hearts above *all* else. The same adviser gave a great explanation of the heart, stating, "It's the essence of who we are."

Our hearts are incredibly important to God.

We may wonder how we *can* guard it. What does that look like?

Here are three ways we can guard our hearts.

1. Guard a heart by accepting truth.

It seems odd to say we can guard our hearts by accepting truth. But it's true. Often, we believe lies and accept them as truth. This leaves our heart unguarded.

There's a reason why a romance novel is the best-selling genre. There's *always* a happy ending. It's a requirement if you want to write such a book. But that's fantasy and not realistic. We're never guaranteed a happily ever after and we shouldn't live in a fantasy world regarding those we love.

Sometimes, we live in what we *want* to be true instead of actual truth.

They say love is blind and its often true. We wear blinders to the behaviors of those we love. We don't want to believe our spouse would cheat on us. We don't want to believe our child would do anything that would get them into trouble with the law. We may idolize our family life, church life, or our marriage. Believing what we want instead of the truth.

> *They exchanged the truth about God for a lie, and worshipped and served created things rather than the Creator—who is forever praised. Amen. (Romans 1:25)*

When God tears down an idol and the walls of a lie come tumbling down, truth remains. God is elevated in our lives, and we see reality. It'll probably be painful.

People will disappoint us in many ways, but God will never leave us in our times of trouble. The truth is He will be glorified when the truth is revealed because we'll know He alone can be trusted, and He loves us more than anyone else ever will.

Our worship will be more genuine because we know Him in a better way. And trust Him in a way we never knew possible.

> *Then you will know the truth, and the truth will set you free. (John 8:32)*

2. Guard a heart with boundaries.

What exactly is a boundary?

Boundaries are our own safety guardrails. Not walls built up out of self-protection.

Think of the guardrails we see along highways; they keep us from running off the road and careening down a steep cliff.

Our boundaries are a guide for us to keep us safe—spiritually, emotionally, and possibly physically.

There's major road construction near me on the interstate. It's dangerous driving through the construction zone due to the improvements in process. There are already a couple of crosses along the road where some drivers have died in car accidents. It can be confusing for drivers who are unfamiliar with the area. The lanes have been repainted in this stretch of highway and careful attention is necessary to navigate the changes.

When we set personal boundaries, it's similar to new lanes being painted on an interstate. Confusing for travelers but necessary for improvements. They are different for each of us. The questions are simple. What is acceptable to me? Does it align with my spiritual walk?

If something is no longer acceptable with us, then we must set a boundary.

Like the new, confusing lanes of road construction near me; eventually they'll turn into a nice new highway, and everyone will benefit.

> *Be on your guard; stand firm in the faith; be courageous; be strong. Do everything in love. (1 Corinthians 16:13)*

3. Guard a heart by seeking God.

When we seek God, we're guarding our hearts.

He is our ultimate protection. When we spend time in prayer, study, and worship, He's glorified. We naturally want to build walls around a broken heart but surrounding ourselves with God is the best protection possible.

> *Do not be overcome by evil, but overcome evil with good. (Romans 12:21)*

The more we read the Bible and study what God has to say about things, the more the Word of God becomes part of us. Literally. Through the power of the Holy Spirit, our minds are renewed and when our thoughts change, our hearts do too.

> *Do not conform to the pattern of this world, but be transformed by the renewing of your mind. Then you will be able to test and approve what God's will is—his good, pleasing, and perfect will. (Romans 12:2)*

Here are ways to know a heart is guarded.

- It's humble and teachable.
- It's an honest and forgiving heart.
- It's full of compassion for others.
- It seeks God and desires His will.

If we have a few of these things churning within us, our heart is being protected.

We don't want to let our guard down though.

Continue seeking Him with constant surrender. Put into practice what we learn from His word. He is with us. And He loves our precious hearts.

> *Whatever you have learned or received or heard from me, or seen in me—put it into practice. And the God of peace will be with you. (Philippians 4:9)*

CROSS MY HEART

***This article was first published 4/27/2022 on Crosswalk.com

• CHAPTER 22 •

Six Reasons to Trust the Clay of Your Troubles in the Potter's Hands

Sooner or later, we'll have trouble in life.

We may find ourselves out of work and financially strapped. We may become depressed about a rough patch in our marriage or an end to one. We may lose someone we love and our hearts are crushed.

But God doesn't leave us during difficult times. He doesn't forsake us when we're broken or troubled. He is the potter, and we are the clay.

I learned an interesting fact about forming clay from watching a children's program. The host mentioned something about the pottery-making process that struck me spiritually.

"The clay is softened and able to be molded through the *warmth* of the potter's hands."

Warmth of the potter's hands?

Clay can't soften itself or form a shape on its own. The warm hands of the potter touching the clay is what causes it to soften. Then it can be formed and shaped into something useful such as a bowl or some other piece of pottery.

Honestly, I never once thought about the warmth of the potter's hands. But after this children's program, I saw God as the potter and us as the clay in a whole new light.

> *Yet you, LORD, are our Father. We are the clay, you are the potter; we are all the work of your hand. (Isaiah 64:8)*

It's a beautiful scripture. But even more so through the lens of *warmth* and God's love for us.

Here are six reasons to trust the clay of your troubles in the Potter's hands.

1. God made us and He doesn't make mistakes.

If you've held a newborn baby, you can't help but wonder at the miracle of it all. We count fingers and toes and marvel at creation. Just thinking about how the brain or eyes work is incredible. *How did He make these things?*

Even though babies seem perfect to us, they aren't. They will make mistakes in life as we all do.

It's not easy when we realize we've made a big mistake. We may try to quickly fix it, beat ourselves up over it, or pretend it didn't happen.

Trouble can come from the mistakes we make.

Everyone makes them but God does not. His ways are perfect. He's in control and knows what He's doing and why. We must trust His spiritual molding process with us, knowing His works are wonderful and full of purpose.

> *I praise you because I am fearfully and wonderfully made; your works are wonderful, I know that full well. (Psalm 139:14)*

2. God is a planner.

Our intentions in life don't always go according to plan.

I spent several years moving from one job to the next. Every place I went to work—I got laid off. They were making department cuts or budget cuts. I couldn't get settled anywhere. It was discouraging. I started keeping a plastic grocery bag in my desk everywhere I went because I never trusted how long I'd be there.

It's frustrating when our plans don't work out and it's out of our control.

But God is never out of control and His plans work out the way **He** intended. We might think things aren't going right and wonder, *how can this be God's plan?*

His plans will fall into place at the right time and are for *our* good.

I have to add that I ended up working for a fantastic company but it took many years of moving from job to job until I finally got there. Now, I see the training I received during those unsettling years working jobs that didn't last—paid off in the long run. I now use most everything in my current job that I learned along the way in all of those temporary positions I *wanted* to be permanent.

I'm so thankful God moved me where He wanted me instead of my own plans working out. I'm in a much better place.

> *"For I know the plans I have for you," declares the LORD, "plans to prosper you and not to harm you, plans to give you hope and a future. (Jeremiah 29:11)*

3. God loves us.

Sometimes, our hearts develop a callus or two from the pressures of life. It might become hardened as a way of protection from pain and pressure. That's when God may break out the chisel and begin to carve away those rough places that have built up over time.

The *making* can sometimes feel like *breaking*.

It can seem as if God is being tough on us as we go through the chiseling process but it's necessary to make our hearts tender again. He does it because of His deep love for us.

> *The LORD is close to the brokenhearted and saves those who are crushed in spirit. (Psalm 34:18)*

4. God knows our troubles.

Our trouble may cause us to believe nobody knows how we feel. It can seem we're going through distressing times alone.

But as God's children, we never go through anything alone. And God knows how the trouble makes us feel. There's nothing any of us go through that He doesn't already know about and understand.

We can go to Him with any problem in life. Period.

> *For we do not have a high priest who is unable to empathize with our weaknesses, but we have one who has been tempted in every way, just as we are—yet he did not sin.* (Hebrews 4:15)

5. God finishes His work.

If you're anything like me, you might have left some things *unfinished* in life.

I admit I have rough drafts of several manuscripts that need major work but it's overwhelming, so they remain undone. I regret I never finished college. Honestly, I could make a list of tasks I'd like to complete before I die.

But God doesn't leave His work undone. He finishes what He starts. Not only does He finish but He makes lovely art. We are His handiwork. What He started in us, He will finish. Molding and forming us into something useful. Something better than we were before.

> *Being confident of this, that he who began a good work in you will carry it on to completion until the day of Christ Jesus. (Philippians 1:6)*

6. He is worthy.

God made us and He doesn't make mistakes. He loves us. He plans perfectly. He finishes His work and knows how we feel. He's *completely* trustworthy.

We will have trouble of one kind or another. There's no getting around it.

Trust the One who loves us so much He won't leave us the way He found us. We were cold, hard clay until the warm hands of the potter began His work in our lives.

Will we have troubles? Yes, we sure will.

Best to place them in the loving, warm hands of the Potter.

> *"I have told you these things, so that in me you may have peace. In this world you will have trouble. But take heart! I have overcome the world." (John 16:33)*

***This article was first published 10/20/2020 on Crosswalk.com

• CHAPTER 23 •

To Err Is Human

Nobody's perfect.

I've made some big mistakes in life. I've wished I could turn back the hands of time and fix things more often than I'd like to admit. But, unfortunately, we have to live with our mistakes. Sometimes, we can only hope and pray for forgiveness from others.

You may have heard the statement, "None of us are getting out of here alive." (Nanea Hoffman) The same is true with forgiveness. We aren't getting through life without needing it from someone. And none of us are getting through life without experiencing the need to forgive someone else for pain they've caused us.

Sometimes, we wait for an apology that *never* comes. Still, we need to forgive even when the offender doesn't make an effort to make things right. That can be tough especially if the pain is deep. But it is possible to forgive and it's the beginning of healing.

Most of all, we need forgiveness from God.

Does the Bible Actually Say "To Err Is Human" or "To Forgive Is Divine"?

The Bible doesn't say *"To err is human"* or *"To forgive is divine"* in those exact words but it does say it in *other* words.

Everyone born into this world inherited a fallen human nature from our ancestors—Adam and Eve. We will sin and make mistakes. No matter how hard we try to avoid it, we can't help it. We are human, after all, and prone "to err."

> *Surely, I was sinful at birth, sinful from the time my mother conceived me. (Psalm 51:5)*

As Christians, we receive the wonderful, powerful Holy Spirit. He helps us forgive when we find it painfully difficult to do so. To forgive through the power of the Holy Spirit is "divine."

> *Peter replied, "Repent, and be baptized, every one of you, in the name of Jesus Christ, for the forgiveness of your sins. And you will receive the gift of the Holy Spirit." (Acts 2:38)*

Origin of the Statement *"To Err Is Human to Forgive Is Divine"*

The statement *"To err is human; to forgive, divine"* is originally from a poem written in 1711 by the English poet Alexander Pope titled *An Essay on Criticism, Part II*. The lengthy poem is a discussion and critique of the art of poetry and poetry readers of his day.

The author explains that while we all make mistakes; we should aspire to do as God does and show mercy and forgiveness to others.

What Does Jesus Say about Human Error and Forgiveness?

In the book of Matthew, Jesus speaks of how we sometimes err.

> *Now then, at the resurrection, whose wife will she be of the seven, since all of them were married to her?" Jesus replied, "You are in **error** because you do not know the scriptures or the power of God. At the resurrection people will neither marry nor be given in marriage; they will be like the angels in heaven." (Matthew 22:28–30)*

In this passage, Jesus is replying to a question about marriage. But the answer He gives is true in most everything for us. We might err because we don't *know* the scriptures the way we should and maybe we don't really *know* His great power.

Also, in Matthew, Jesus speaks of forgiveness.

> *For if you forgive other people when they sin against you, your heavenly Father will also forgive you. But if you do not forgive others their sins, your Father will not forgive your sins. (Matthew 6:14–15)*

And, in Mark, Jesus advises: *And when you stand praying, if you hold anything against anyone, forgive them, so that your Father in heaven may forgive you your sins." (Mark 11:25)*

Holding onto "unforgiveness" can cause problems in our relationship with God. We're commanded to forgive others because He's forgiven us.

Four Scriptures that Highlight Our Error and Forgiveness

We're completely unaware of some of our own errors and being *blessed* to be forgiven.

1. *But who can discern their own errors? Forgive my hidden faults. (Psalm 19:12)*

2. *Blessed is the one whose transgressions are forgiven; whose sins are covered. (Psalm 32:1)*

3. *I will cleanse them from all the sin they have committed against me and will forgive all their sins of rebellion against me. (Jeremiah 33:8)*

4. *For all have sinned and fall short of the glory of God. (Romans 3:23)*

Why Is It "Divine" to Forgive?

As Christians, we're asked to forgive the way God forgave us. He lavished grace, mercy, and love upon us and washed our sins away through the blood of His beloved Son.

How can we ever forgive in such a way?

It can be easy to **say** we forgive someone. The problem is we can't forget. Our nature is not to forgive but to get even with the person who hurt us.

We might struggle day after day to put the pain and trauma behind us but it lingers in our minds and hearts. We can't seem to forget even though we've verbally forgiven them. We may find ourselves begging God to help us forgive because we find we're unable to do it in our own power.

God is the only one capable of forgiving *and* forgetting.

> *"I, even I, am he who blots out your transgressions, for my own sake, and remembers your sins no more." (Isaiah 43:35)*

> *As far as the east is from the west, so far has he removed our transgressions from us. (Psalm 103:12)*

But, each day we struggle is a day we can grow closer to God by seeking His help. We can put the trouble of our inability to truly forgive into His powerful hands.

Then we're able to forgive through the power of the Holy Spirit. It's a beautiful thing when forgiveness comes from the heart.

Four Things Christians Should Remember about the Statement *"To Err Is Human, to Forgive Is Divine"*

1. We all mess up and need forgiveness.

2. Forgiving can be hard and forgetting is not easy.

3. We can forgive someone through the divine power of the Holy Spirit.

4. When we forgive others as God forgave us, we're reflecting traits of our Savior by extending grace and mercy.

They say time heals all wounds. I don't know if that's true but it does help. Sadly, it can take years to get through some things in life.

When we become a Christian, God forgives *once* for all of our sins because of His deep love for us. We may find ourselves trying to forgive someone over and over again because we're incapable of forgiving difficult things in life without the help of the Holy Spirit.

Know that we *all* make mistakes. We might cause someone deep pain or vice versa. We may be disappointed in the worst way and it can seem impossible to forgive in our *own* strength. But through the power of the Holy Spirit, we can forgive because He forgave us.

> *Blessed is the one whose transgressions are forgiven; whose sins are covered. (Psalm 32:1)*

****This article was first published 4/13/2020 on Crosswalk.com*

• CHAPTER 24 •

Can Anyone Really Be above Reproach?

IF YOU'RE INVOLVED IN a church in some way, you may have heard the word *reproach* mentioned in passing. Maybe you didn't give the word much thought. But it usually comes up when new leaders are being considered for positions within the church.

We hear within the Christian community that church leaders, or deacons, should be *"above reproach."* What exactly does that even mean?

What Does *Reproach* Mean?

The definition for *reproach* according to Miriam–Webster's Dictionary is "an expression of rebuke or disapproval . . . to express disappointment in or displeasure with (a person) for conduct that is blameworthy or in need of amendment."

Basically, *reproach* means to discredit, disgrace, or disapprove.

To be *"above reproach"* would mean a person is blameless.

Where in the Bible Are Christians Called to Be Above Reproach?

One scripture where this comes from is 1 Timothy 3:1–7.

> *Here is a trustworthy saying: Whoever aspires to be an overseer desires a noble task. Now the overseer is to be above reproach, faithful to his wife, temperate, self-controlled, respectable, hospitable, able to teach, not given to drunkenness, not violent but gentle, not quarrelsome, not a lover of money. He must manage his own family well and see that his children obey him, and he must do so in a manner worthy of full respect. (If anyone does not know how to manage his own family, how can he take care of God's church?) He must not be a recent convert, or he may become conceited and fall under the same judgment as the devil. He must also have a good reputation with outsiders, so that he will not fall into disgrace and into the devil's trap.*

Often this scripture is the standard for appointing church leaders, deacons, and elders. A similar scripture is found in Titus 1:5–9.

> *The reason I left you in Crete was that you might put in order what was left unfinished and appoint elders in every town, as I directed you. An elder must be blameless, faithful to his wife, a man whose children believe and are not open to the charge of being wild and disobedient. Since an overseer manages God's household, he must be blameless—not overbearing, not quick-tempered, not given to drunkenness, not violent, not pursuing dishonest gain. Rather, he must be hospitable, one who loves what is good, who is self-controlled, upright, holy, and disciplined. He must hold firmly*

> to the trustworthy message as it has been taught, so that he can encourage others by sound doctrine and refute those who oppose it.

This is a high standard for Christians, or anybody to be honest.

It excludes some from leadership positions in ministry who may have made mistakes early in life or have been divorced. Even though they may have an incredible relationship with God, they're unable to serve in leadership positions in some churches due to this high standard.

In all honesty, it seems unfair. God has worked miraculously in the lives of many people. It seems a shame those strong Christians with a deep love for God, are not allowed to hold positions of leadership in some church bodies.

We all make mistakes in life but especially in our youth. We may have married someone we shouldn't have and were unable to make it work. Is it right that this person who made a mistake early in life is considered unfit to be a leader or deacon?

We're all human and imperfect. If a person thinks they're without any faults, then they have at least one problem. *Pride.*

Nobody is perfect and all sin.

We may find someone "above reproach" by our standards because we can't see inside another person's mind or spirit to see who they really are or what they may be dealing with in their personal lives. God sees the heart and knows our every thought.

Truth is, those in leadership roles in many churches have unseen issues in their lives. Just because they have a good reputation in the community doesn't mean they're blameless. Some people are good at covering up bad behavior, so others are unaware.

How Can Christians Answer This Call Today?

Christians are filled with the Holy Spirit. He convicts us when we're in the wrong. He guides us to do the right things in God's sight. He teaches us so we will grow more like Jesus.

Unfortunately, the same way we make mistakes in our younger years, we also make mistakes in our spiritual youth.

We're just learning to follow the guidance of the Holy Spirit and sometimes fail. We teeter between flesh and spirit trying to find our way. We act impulsively out of flesh at times and then later feel the conviction of the Holy Spirit showing us the error of our ways.

We will eventually learn not to repeat the mistake by yielding ourselves to God and listening to the Holy Spirit.

Spiritual maturity takes quite a while to achieve. Even some older Christians are not spiritually mature. They are little spiritual children walking around the earth in aged bodies.

However, with the power of the Holy Spirit within us, we can strive to be above reproach. Here are a few ways we can make those efforts.

Honor God with our lives.

> *Do you not know that your bodies are temples of the Holy Spirit, who is in you, whom you have received from God? You are not your own; you were bought at a price. Therefore, honor God with your bodies. (1 Corinthians 6:19–20)*

Forgive others even when it's impossible to forget.

> *Bear with each other and forgive one another if any of you has a grievance against someone. Forgive as the Lord forgave you. (Colossians 3:13)*

Love others the way God has asked us to love others—like He does.

> *A new command I give you: Love one another. As I have loved you, so you must love one another. (John 13:34)*

Within our own strength, we will struggle to be blameless. We're human and imperfect. We mess up. But when we do, we should seek forgiveness and admit the wrong. Then make valiant efforts to make things right.

God, in His great goodness, shows us grace upon grace, and mercy beyond our comprehension. His forgiveness—a soothing balm to our souls.

> *Out of his fullness we have all received grace in place of grace already given. (John 1:16)*

Who is truly blameless?

Jesus.

Such a high priest truly meets our need—one who is holy, blameless, pure, set apart from sinners, exalted above the heavens. Unlike the other high priests, he does not need to offer sacrifices day after day, first for his own sins, and then for the sins of the people. He sacrificed for their sins once for all when he offered himself. (Hebrews 7:26–27)

***This article was first published 3/10/2021 on Crosswalk.com

• CHAPTER 25 •

Do Christians Care More about Looking Good than Being Good?

"Every old barn could use a little paint!"

Those words were spoken by a pastor at a church where I once worked. I cracked up because he was referring to women wearing makeup. I'd never heard a pastor say such a thing. Being raised by a preacher of a small conservative church, I was allowed to wear some light makeup but he didn't like it much. From time to time, he made me aware I was wearing too much.

I'd love to blame it on growing up in the eighties when pop music stars like Michael Jackson and Madonna were all the rage. But truthfully, I like to look good. At least, I like to look my *best*. Though, I'm sure when I was young, I did wear too much eye shadow from time to time.

It's one thing to want to look good physically but it's a whole other issue when we desire to look good spiritually in front of others *instead* of actually being good.

We can only truly be good through Jesus Christ. As Christians, God is constantly working on us making us more like His Son. He's changing our ways to His ways. Making us like Jesus through the power of the Holy Spirit residing within us when we become a Christian.

The desire to be good spiritually is really a good thing because it stems from our efforts to be obedient to God. We want to please our Father and represent Him well on Earth. The need to *look good* in front of other Christians spiritually is an issue of our flesh.

But we're human and this is one of our struggles.

Here are a few things to consider about looking good and being good.

1. God sees the heart.

> "I the LORD search the heart and examine the mind, to reward each person according to their conduct, according to what their deeds deserve." (Jeremiah 17:10)

We focus on beauty, happiness, and whatever is appealing to our eyes and makes us feel good.

God searches our hearts and *examines* our minds. He sees our good and bad attitudes. He *knows* why we do the things we do when we may have no idea.

Many have most likely heard the statement, *"What goes around comes around,"* or some version of the same sentiment. Some believe in karma, which is basically the same thing. But God is the ultimate authority on getting what we deserve according to our actions.

What we see in people is not what God sees when He looks at us. We may be able to get a glimpse of the heart of another person by how they live their life or treat others but we're limited in what we see. We can't read minds or know the true intentions of another person's actions. But God does.

He knows us inside and out. Every detail is clear. The "what and why" of our every move is known by Him.

While we appreciate a person by their appearance many times and judge them in this way, God gazes deeply into our hearts.

> *But the LORD said to Samuel, "Do not consider his appearance or his height, for I have rejected him. The LORD does not look at the things people look at. People look at the outward appearance, but the LORD looks at the heart." (1 Samuel 16:7)*

2. God knows our thoughts.

I don't know about you but I'm glad my thoughts aren't in a bubble above my head for the whole world to see. We think about lots of stuff *best* kept to ourselves.

In our thoughts, we ponder doing right and wrong. We wonder about our own actions and the actions of others. Why did they do this or why didn't I do that?

Our *flesh* is vivid in our thoughts. We wrestle spiritually with it on a daily basis because we're human.

God knows how we think and why. It's interesting that God made us with the ability to think yet He perceives our thoughts before we may even realize what they might mean?

He's familiar with our nature and understands us when we do things that make no sense or have selfish thoughts and ideas about our lives or the lives of others.

Thank goodness, He loves us enough to make a way for us through the sacrifice of His Son, Jesus. Just our *thoughts* are enough to get us into trouble spiritually without the actions that most oftentimes follow those thoughts.

> *You know when I sit and when I rise; you perceive my thoughts from afar. (Psalm 139:2)*

3. God knows our intentions.

There's an old saying about the path to *somewhere* being paved with good intentions.

The reason is we justify our actions by saying we have good intentions. Maybe we even believe it. Sometimes our intentions *seem* good to us. But we may have unknown ulterior motives working behind the scenes in our own minds and hearts. It could be a guise to do something we really shouldn't do veiled in goodness.

We like to keep up good appearances especially in front of other Christians. Heaven forbid someone discovers our hidden sin.

Once, I was in a *serious* meeting with another Christian. Instead of apologizing for bad behavior and making things right, this person felt the need to lie *repeatedly* to look better. Appearances were so important to this person, that actually lying to other Christians (and God) seemed to be the better choice as long as they *looked good in front of others*.

Human nature at its *finest*.

Sadly, we have no choice but to deal with this type of behavior with other Christians at times, because of our nature. Often, our first instinct is the one of our flesh—*not* the spirit.

As we grow as a Christian, we become more inclined toward spirit *first* instead of flesh. But our spiritual growth takes a long time and many mistakes are made along the way. Thank goodness for God's great grace and mercy toward us as we grow up.

He loves us enough to give us stress tests in areas of life until we make the connection between our flesh behavior and what's right in His sight. He will continue to test us until we "get it" and *change* our behavior.

> *Search me, God, and know my heart; test me and know my anxious thoughts. (Psalm 139:23)*

God knows *why* we do the things we do. He knows if our intentions are good or if they're bad and born from selfish motives. He knows if we're trying to *look* good instead of *be* good.

Of course, every old barn could use a little paint! A freshening up never did any harm. Our spirits also need to be refreshed. Digging deeper into our faith, deeper into God's Word, and deeper in our relationship with Him will not only make us look good spiritually but will actually be good in His sight.

We can't go wrong seeking God and His will for our lives.

> *"For my thoughts are not your thoughts, neither are your ways my ways," declares the LORD. (Isaiah 55:8)*

***This article was first published 4/26/2021 on Crosswalk.com

• CHAPTER 26 •

What Is the Significance of Mount Moriah in the Bible?

Mount Moriah is a holy site in Jerusalem and an important place for Christians. Most of us have heard it mentioned in sermons or have read about Moriah in our study time. But what is the significance of Mount Moriah in the Bible?

It's tied to some of the most incredible events of obedience recorded in the Bible. We may not see the connection unless it's brought to our attention.

The first mention of Moriah in the Bible is found in Genesis 22, with Abraham and Isaac.

This Bible story is one of the first I remember from childhood. My grandparents had a big family Bible on their coffee table, and I'd thumb through it as a child because of the beautiful artist depictions found inside. The picture of Abraham hovering over his son, who is tied up, with a large knife about to kill him was seared into my brain.

At my young age, I couldn't comprehend foreshadowing and God giving a picture through Abraham and Isaac of a future event to take place. The sacrifice of His only beloved Son, Jesus. I couldn't have begun to understand how God may test us, as Christians, either.

What Is Mount Moriah, and Where Is It Today?

Mount Moriah is a mountain with an elevation of approximately 2,520 feet and found in Jerusalem. It's a good-sized mountain but not super high.

To compare, the elevation of Pikes Peak in the Colorado Rockies is 14,115 feet.

It's considered important to several religions including Christians, Jews, and Muslims.

What Is the Significance of Mount Moriah?

Mount Moriah is the site of several important biblical events.

1. It's the site of the testing of Abraham when God asked him to take the life of his only son, Isaac.

> *Then God said, "Take your son, your only son, whom you love—Isaac—and go to the region of Moriah. Sacrifice him there as a burnt offering on a mountain I will show you." (Genesis 22:2)*

2. It's the same place Solomon built the Temple.

> *Then Solomon began to build the temple of the LORD in Jerusalem on Mount Moriah, where the LORD had appeared to his father David. It was on the threshing floor of Araunah the Jebusite, the place provided by David. (2 Chronicles 3:1)*

3. Scholars believe Mount Moriah is also the place (or nearby) where Jesus was sacrificed on the cross for the sins of the world—Golgotha.

> *Finally Pilate handed him over to them to be crucified. So the soldiers took charge of Jesus. Carrying his own cross, he went out to the place of the Skull (which in Aramaic is called Golgotha). There they crucified him, and with him two others—one on each side and Jesus in the middle. (John 19:16–18)*

In the testing of Abraham, God provided a substitute ram caught in a thicket nearby and Abraham didn't have to literally sacrifice his only, beloved son, Isaac.

> *"Do not lay a hand upon the boy," he said. "Do not do anything to him. Now I know you fear God, because you have not withheld from me your son, your only son." Abraham looked up and there in a thicket he saw a ram caught by its horns. He went over and took the ram and sacrificed it as a burnt offering instead of his son. So Abraham called that place The LORD Will Provide. And to this day it is said,*

"On the mountain of the LORD it will be provided." (Genesis 22:12–14)

But God did **not** provide a substitute for His own beloved Son. Jesus **was** the substitute sacrifice for **us**. The perfect lamb of God.

Why Are the Events of Mount Moriah Important to Us Today?

God doesn't change. The incredible events of Mount Moriah and the lessons they provide are applicable today for our relationship with God.

1. God will test us.

The story with Abraham and Isaac on Mount Moriah is a demonstration of a future event pointing to Jesus and God's plan of salvation for mankind. However, it also reveals how God tests His children.

Our testing will not involve anything quite as dramatic, but it will be difficult because a test is not a true test unless it's hard for us. Maybe God has been working in our lives trying to get us to trust Him regarding money. The test may be that we lose our job.

Will we trust His provision through job loss?

Will we desire His will in our lives even if it involves moving us to another place of employment?

Passing the test will involve peace. We go with the flow of God—*knowing* He has our best interest at heart and is in control of everything.

> *Fear not, for I am with you; do not be dismayed, for I am your God. I will strengthen you and help you; I will uphold you with my righteous right hand. (Isaiah 41:10)*

2. God's timing is perfect.

When Abraham was about to plunge the knife into his son, God provided a ram for the sacrifice instead. God's timing is perfect. The ram happened to be caught in a thicket nearby just when the substitute sacrifice was needed to save the life of his son, Isaac.

God arranged for the ram to be caught in the thicket. He knew Abraham wouldn't take the life of his own beloved son. But Abraham didn't know. He was following through with incredible obedience and faith, willing to do whatever God asked of him.

Our testing is the same. God is all-knowing and has a plan for us to get through the testing he's placed us into. If we lose our job to test our faith in God's provision, He already knows where we'll be employed next.

Maybe we will be paid more money or have better working conditions. Maybe we would have *never* left our employer on our own but through a test of our faith, God moves us to a better place.

Because of His perfect timing, we trust Him more and more.

> *There is a time for everything, and a season for every activity under heavens. (Ecclesiastes 3:1)*

3. God's plan is best.

To be honest, death doesn't seem like a good plan.

We hate it and avoid death for as long as possible. But God sees things differently than we do. (Isaiah 55:8–9)

Death was part of His perfect plan of salvation for us. The death and resurrection of His one and only beloved Son is how He made a way for us to have a right relationship with Him again.

Jesus lived the perfect life none of us are capable of living. He was the fulfillment of the perfect sacrifice required by God that Abraham demonstrated in Genesis with his son, Isaac.

Mount Moriah, where God tested Abraham asking him to sacrifice Isaac, is the same place where Jesus was sacrificed years later as the perfect lamb sacrifice for all mankind.

How perfect are the plans of God?

In our Christian walk, we **will** see God's perfect plans and timing repeatedly in our lives. We may see the new job we end up doing—after we lost the job with God's test in our life—is exactly what we needed at the exact time we needed it. The job just opened, and we were the perfect candidate.

The more we learn this truth about how God works, the easier life is because we know He will not fail us. If things don't go the way we expect, then we wait for His perfect plan and timing.

> *But the plans of the LORD stand firm forever, the purposes of his heart through all generations. (Psalm 33:11)*

Mount Moriah is a *special* place because of the testing of Abraham with his son, Isaac, foreshadowing the redemptive plan of God with His own Son. The building of the Temple by King Solomon. And the crucifixion of God's Son, Jesus—our Savior.

> *Later, knowing that everything had now been finished, and so that scripture would be fulfilled, Jesus said, "I am thirsty." A jar of wine vinegar was there, so they soaked a sponge in it, put the sponge on a stalk of the hyssop plant, and lifted it to Jesus' lips. When he had received the drink, Jesus said, "It is finished." With that, he bowed his head and gave up his spirit. (John 19:28–30)*

***This article was first published 11/03/2021 on Crosswalk.com

• CHAPTER 27 •

How to Start a Prayer

THERE'S NO EXACT WAY we should start a prayer. God wants to hear from us even if we're unsure how to begin.

As Christians, we're in a relationship with an all-knowing God. He loves us more than we can even imagine. Because of Jesus, we can go to God as a loving Father who cares about the smallest details of our lives. He wants us to tell Him about our life struggles and to make our requests known to Him. He *already knows* what we're going through. But sometimes we already know what our own children are going through, too, but we still like to hear about it from them.

It can feel a bit intimidating to pray especially if we've heard others pray who've been doing it for years.

Sometimes, getting started can be a problem if we're a new Christian or new to prayer. Especially, public prayer.

Are There Different Ways to Start a Prayer?

If we look to scripture as our example, we will find some prayers beginning with an acknowledgment of God's authority and power.

> *"Sovereign Lord, remember me. Please, God, strengthen me just once more, and let me with one blow get revenge on the Philistines for my two eyes." (Samson's prayer in Judges 16:28)*

> *"Lord Almighty, if you will only look on your servant's misery and remember me, and not forget your servant but give her a son, then I will give him to the Lord for all the days of his life, and no razor will ever be used on his head." (Hannah's prayer in 1 Samuel 1:9–11)*

I tend to begin prayers with *Heavenly Father* because that's who He is to me.

Starting our prayer with praise is always great because He's worthy of our praise.

> *"Enter his gates with thanksgiving and his courts with praise; give thanks to him and praise his name." (Psalm 100:4)*

What about the Lord's Prayer Model?

When I was young, Dad would sometimes invite me to pray with him and would lead me in the Lord's Prayer. He'd say a line of the prayer and then have me repeat it. This was a great example given to me as a child.

We can't go wrong following the example Jesus gave His disciples when they asked him to teach them to pray.

> *"This, then, is how you should pray: 'Our Father in heaven, hallowed be your name, your kingdom come, your will be done, on earth as it is in heaven. Give us today our daily bread. And forgive us our debts, as we also have forgiven our debtors. And lead us not into temptation, but deliver us from the evil one.'" (Matthew 6:9–13)*

Again, we see the acknowledgment of who God is in the example Jesus gave the disciples. Another word for *hallowed* is *holy*.

It's a great prayer template to follow—not necessarily word for word, but as a guide for our own prayers.

Approaching God with reverence for who He is.

Being yielded to His will here on earth.

Making our requests known to Him.

Asking for forgiveness and help in times of temptation.

Why Does It Matter How We Start a Prayer?

God is perfect, Holy, and just. He always has our best interest at heart. If you know Him, you also know He deserves to be addressed with honor and respect.

It doesn't matter how we choose to address Him as long as we're acknowledging how greatly we respect Him for everything He's done for us. (Some of which we are completely unaware.)

Whatever we request in prayer we need to find a place of balance between our hopes and His will. Asking for what we want but knowing God's way is best. His way may not include exactly what we desire.

Have confidence in God's answer to our prayer even if it's not what we asked for. We want His will in our lives just as it is in heaven.

It's not always God's will to heal a loved one or for us to get a particular job we desire.

There's a popular song about God's unanswered prayers and how they are some of His greatest gifts to us. The truth is our heartfelt prayers don't go *unanswered*. They may *not* be answered in the way we imagined but God will answer them in the best way for us to grow closer to Him. Guaranteed.

> *This is the confidence we have in approaching God: that if we ask anything according to his will, he hears us. And if we know that he hears us—whatever we ask—we know that we have what we asked of him. (1 John 5:14–15)*

What Should Be in the Middle?

When we know God has been merciful toward us and given us great grace, we want to thank Him. It comes naturally when we recognize our need of Jesus. We're thankful for God's perfect plan of salvation prepared for us and our hearts are full of gratefulness.

Often, when we feel drawn to pray, we simply thank Him for everything He's done for us. Then pour our hearts out to God, sharing our burdens with Him.

The middle might be muddled because we may be distressed and that's what has drawn us to pray. We may be brought to tears as we pour out what's weighing on our hearts and minds so heavily, trusting God to take care of our troubles.

> *Do not be anxious about anything, but in every situation, by prayer and petition, with thanksgiving, present your requests to God. And the peace of God, which transcends all understanding, will guard your hearts and your minds in Christ Jesus. (Philippians 4:6–7)*

In our distress, the Holy Spirit may step in and pray on our behalf. Maybe we can't find the words to express our deep sorrow or heartache. Maybe all we can do is weep at the feet of Jesus and release grief.

> *In the same way, the Spirit helps us in our weakness. We do not know what we ought to pray for, but the Spirit himself intercedes for us through wordless groans. And he who searches our hearts knows the mind of the Spirit, because the Spirit intercedes for God's people in accordance with the will of God. (Romans 8:26–27)*

He already knows about our distress but wants us to go to Him with everything. The good, the bad, and the *ugly*.

How Should a Prayer End?

Have you ever heard a public prayer that goes on and on until we wonder if it will ever end?

People begin drifting, peeking around the room, and checking their watches.

Instead of simply speaking to God from their heart, the one praying seems to be seeking attention from others for their ability to continue a long-winded prayer. It's a turnoff to many, even Jesus.

It's important to have a humble spirit when approaching God.

> *But when you pray, go into your room, close the door and pray to your Father, who is unseen. Then your Father, who sees what is done in secret, will reward you. And when you pray, do not keep on babbling like pagans, for they think they will be heard because of their many words. Do not be like them, for your Father knows what you need before you ask him. (Matthew 6:6–8)*

A heartfelt prayer should end almost the same as it begins. Instead of praising the Father for who He is, we honor God's Son—Jesus.

We often hear prayers end with some variation of *"In the name of Jesus, Amen."*

There's no better name to pray through. His name is powerful, mighty, and full of authority. Making our humble requests known to God through the powerful name of Jesus Christ honors Him and shows our trust is placed fully in Him.

Truly, God wants us to go to Him and hears us when we pray.

> *Rejoice always, pray continually, give thanks in all circumstances; for this is God's will for you in Christ Jesus. (1 Thessalonians 5:16–18)*

***This article was first published 1/6/2021 on Crosswalk.com

• CHAPTER 28 •

How to Explain What the Holy Spirit Is

Recently, a conversation took place at dinner about the children of Israel and how they ended up in Egypt as slaves. As I shared the story of Joseph and his brothers, and how they initially found themselves in Egypt, one of my sons had his phone out and googled something I said to find out if I was right.

It had been a while since I'd recalled those particular biblical highlights, so it caused me to question myself but when Google proved it true, then my recollection was good as gold.

Google is a useful tool and I use it often. But having a search engine working for us doesn't compare to having the Holy Spirit *working* within us.

Some seekers, may be unfamiliar and might wonder—*What is the* ***Holy Spirit?***

The first thing to know is the Holy Spirit is a ***Who***. He's a Spirit. The ***Holy*** Spirit. The Third Person in the Trinity.

God is three persons—Father, Son, and Holy Spirit. They're all God just in different forms.

It can be hard to wrap our minds around such a thing. But the best explanation of the Trinity I've heard uses water as the example. There's water, ice, and steam. They're all water. But in different forms. It helps a bit to think of it in that way.

We can tell a lot about those in our lives who *love* and care about us by what they ***do***. They prove they love us deeply with their actions. Sometimes in sacrificial ways. They want the best for us even if it means giving up something on their part.

God loves us so much. He sent Jesus to make a way for us to have right relationship with Him again. Jesus willingly went to the cross for us. When we become a Christian and surrender our lives to His will, we receive the Holy Spirit. He indwells us and fulfills an amazing role.

Then His incredible work begins in our lives as He transforms us and makes us more and more like Jesus.

Here are eight things the Holy Spirit *does* in the life of a Christian.

1. He indwells us.

> *Do you not know that your bodies are temples of the Holy Spirit, who **is in you**, whom you have received from God? You are not your own: you were bought at a price. Therefore, honor God with your bodies. (1 Corinthians 6:19–20)*

When we surrender our lives to God, our physical body becomes the temple of God and the Holy Spirit dwells within us for the rest of our natural lives.

2. He teaches and reminds us.

> *But the Advocate, the Holy Spirit, whom the Father will send in my name, will teach you all things and will remind you of everything I have said to you. (John 14:26)*

When we read the Bible with the Holy Spirit within us, it makes a lot of sense and is easier to comprehend. He opens our eyes as we read and teaches us through scripture then later when needed, He reminds us about what God said.

3. He encourages us.

> *Then the church throughout Judea, Galilee, and Samaria enjoyed a time of peace and was strengthened. Living in the fear of the Lord and encouraged by the Holy Spirit, it increased in numbers. (Acts 9:31)*

When we're a Christian, we *are* the church. It's not just a building on the street corner with stained glass windows. It's the people who follow God.

The truth is sometimes the road will get bumpy. We don't stop having problems just because we've become a Christian. Thank God for giving us the Holy Spirit. He's with us through everything—the good, the bad, and the ugly. And He *encourages* us to continue trusting Him in *all* things.

4. He guides us.

> *The two of them, sent on their way by the Holy Spirit, went down to Seleucia and sailed from there to Cyprus. (Acts 13:4)*

As we grow spiritually, we'll have more insight to the guidance of the Holy Spirit. He nudges us in the direction we should go in our lives and helps us make difficult decisions.

He lets us know when its time to change jobs, move, or make a major change in our life when we seek Him and surrender our decisions to Him. We need to be in balance with our wants and His will. Okay with whatever happens trusting *Him* to lead the way.

5. He warns us.

> *I only know that in every city the Holy Spirit warns me that prison and hardships are facing me. (Acts 20:23)*

There's not much better than someone giving us a heads-up. Especially, when it's the Person who knows everything. He sees our future and what's coming our way when we may be completely clueless.

When God gives us a warning, we better listen. It may not change anything but He loves us enough to let us know some things in advance.

6. He gives us hope.

> *May the God of hope fill you with all joy and peace as you trust in him, so that you may overflow with hope by the power of the Holy Spirit. (Romans 15:13)*

The Holy Spirit is powerful in our lives. So many good things come from Him.

Sometimes, we just need some hope as we endure the hardships of life. But as we go through life trusting God more and more through the trials we face, we're filled with joy and peace. Because He proves Himself to be completely trustworthy.

7. He tells us truth.

> *"I have much more to say to you, more than you can now bear. But when he, the Spirit of truth, comes, he will guide you into all the truth. He will not speak on his own; he will speak only what he hears, and he will tell you what is yet to come. (John 16:12–13)*

The Spirit of truth guides us into all truth. The *whole* thing.

I love this so much.

8. He helps us pray.

> *In the same way, the Spirit helps us in our weakness. We do not know what we ought to pray for, but the Spirit himself intercedes for us through wordless groans. (Romans 8:26)*

Often, we don't have words. We're overwhelmed with a situation whether it's death, depression, financial struggles, or any hard thing in life. We hit our knees beside our beds and collapse.

We don't even know how to express ourselves. We can only sigh or groan because we're desperate for God to listen and *help* us. And the Holy Spirit will intercede for us when we're incapable of speaking for ourselves.

There are so many more things He does for us including drawing us to Himself, revealing Jesus, bestowing spiritual gifts, and convicting us of sin in our lives.

Our compassionate, loving God never leaves us because He's dwelling within us. He goes where we go. He knows our thoughts and intentions even when we don't even know them. He works within us to help us turn from sin toward Him.

Always loving us. Always lavishing us with grace and mercy with our best interest at heart. Always.

> *And you also were included in Christ when you heard the message of truth, the gospel of your salvation. When you believe, you were marked in him with a seal, the promised Holy Spirit, who is a deposit guaranteeing our inheritance until the redemption of those who are God's possession—to the praise of his glory. (Ephesians 1:13–14)*

***This article was first published 1/16/2023 on Crosswalk.com

• CHAPTER 28 •

White Trash

IN THE SPRING OF 2015, some beautiful red tulips bloomed near the house we were renting. They're my favorite flower and I needed a new cover photo for social media so an idea was born. Tulips will brighten up my page!

I noticed the barn in the field behind the flowers and lay down on the ground to get the perfect shot. Tulips bursting with colors with a barn behind it. I loved the photo! I soon uploaded it and got tons of lovely comments. Many friends suggested I frame a copy.

Instead of framing a copy, I had a canvas print made to hang on the wall. It was perfect.

Soon, I got a new job with a large, nice office. A coworker suggested I get a larger canvas of the photo to hang above the file cabinets. There was a reimbursement (up to a certain amount) for office decor. Ooh la la!

Before long, I had a lovely, large canvas hanging above my file cabinets to brighten up my new office space.

With the larger print, I noticed something in the background. It was behind the tulips, in the gravel driveway, in front of the barn. It was white. It looked like *trash*.

Our older sons parked back there. It appeared to be a wadded up fast-food bag from Sonic or McDonald's right in the middle of my beautiful tulip photo.

Too late to take another photo. I hadn't noticed the trash when I got excited about the tulips then decided to lay on the ground and capture the barn in the background. The tulips were gone by the time I noticed the trash.

These days, the large canvas is hanging in a new office at my current employer. I see the trash and point it out when I get compliments on the tulip photo. Because it's okay if there is a little trash in the background.

The reality is we all have some trash in our backgrounds. Things we wish weren't there. Things we wish others didn't know or see. Things we wish we could erase.

But we can't change it. By the time we bloom into the person God has called us to be, the trash is a good reminder. We're not the same person we once were. God has *changed* us for the better. But we don't want to forget where we've come from. It makes us thankful for what God has done.

There's *definitely* some white trash in my background. And I'm okay with that.

• CHAPTER 29 •

I Got You

I give them eternal life, and they shall never perish; no one will snatch them out of my hand. (John 10:28)

MY YOUNGEST SON CAME home one day telling me a wild story about his day and how he ended up having to ask his good friend for some help in a tricky situation. *"I got you,"* his friend said and quickly came to my son's rescue.

The phrase his friend used has become common these days among the younger generation.

Something about it just **feels** good. Its almost like loyalty intertwined with love *combined* with knowing we can count on this friend in times of trouble no matter what. *They have our back.*

Not all friendships are this way though.

Some people we think are friends are not really friends at all. They're acquaintances. They're fellow church members. They're coworkers.

We consider them to be our friends. But we may discover when times get tough or our paths don't cross regularly anymore attending the same church or working at the same company, we lose tabs on each other. The friendship fizzles.

Having a true friend in life is priceless. They are gifts to us, for sure. They should be cherished and loved deeply. They are also few and far between. *Sadly.*

But we have a **true** friend in *Jesus.*

He's got us and He's not letting go no matter what. He's there for us in the best of times and the worst times. Never wavering in His affection for us. Never giving up on us because our paths don't cross in familiar places anymore.

I got you.

No truer words could be spoken of His love for us. He is loyalty intertwined with love combined with knowing we can count on Him in times of trouble no matter what.

I love how He holds us tight in His grip. No one will snatch us from His hand.

The irony is He **gripped us** with His arms stretched out on the cross. He gave His life to hold us tight.

• CHAPTER 30 •

Middle-Aged Mama Moment

MIDDLE AGE COMES WITH some good things and some sad things.

Having some freedom is nice. Doing things without the concern of a little one 24/7 is a relief.

But the **same** thing is also one of the sad things about this stage of life.

A while back, I crossed paths with a young mother heading into Walmart with her three young children. A baby sat on her hip, while she held the hand of a smaller child, and led another one who was old enough to walk beside her. She smiled from ear to ear wrangling her children into the store. I smiled because she reminded me of my daughter-in-law with her young children. Just as I passed her, I heard someone yell, "Mama!" I glanced farther down the parking lot and saw my middle son (whose wife I'd just been thinking about) waving wildly at me. He was helping get the kids out of the car as his wife put the youngest in a stroller. I waved at them, popped my trunk, and started loading my groceries while my son took care of his own family.

As I placed the bags in the car a thought crossed my mind.

> *Not very long ago he would've been helping me load groceries into my car.*

Instead of helping his mom like the good boy he had been growing up, he was helping his wife like the good husband he is now.

My heart hurt. *Can I turn back time and enjoy him as my young son again just for a little while?* They made their way toward me as my middle-aged heart ached to be a mom once again. "I was just thinking of you guys!" I said as my sweet granddaughter ran toward me and gave me a hug. After a brief chat, they made their way into the store. I closed my trunk and headed home. I'm not gonna lie . . . I shed some tears before I got there.

It's strange to be in a phase of life where I'm proud of the men my sons have become, but I want my little boys back. I want them to unload my groceries and eat cookie dough meant to be used for cookies. I want to do their laundry and gripe that they won't put it away. Being a mama is such a wonderful thing but sometimes it's hard to realize you can't keep the *moments* forever.

Those moments that seemed ordinary at the time are gone before you know it. You can't relive them. You can only **remember** them. Of course, there are *new* wonderful moments with sweet grandchildren running to you for a hug. I know I need to cherish them because they'll grow up way too fast.

But oh my, some of these moments in my middle-aged life are kinda painful.

> *Start children off on the way they should go, and even when they are old they will not turn from it. (Proverbs 22:6)*

• CHAPTER 31 •

The Gift of a Boy

MY YOUNGEST SON, JOSEPH, wrapped gifts and placed this one under the tree for me. Wrapped in camouflage gift wrap with matching duct tape. He even made sure he used a gift tag with a deer on it. *Pure boy.*

What I love more than anything is that he signed his nickname he claims not to like. He even told us when he was young not to call him "JT" because his nickname was "Camaro." We humored him and called him *Camaro* for a little while but it never really stuck. *Pure boy.*

God made sure when we received all three of our boys, we'd have no idea what he'd wrapped up and given us in the form of a little boy.

Even though Joseph wrapped the Christmas gift in camouflage, wrote my name on it, and placed it under the tree—he is truly the gift to me.

I had no idea what the gift box contained, he made sure of that. I thought it was a cardboard box he saved and placed the gift inside to disguise the true present. He didn't want me guessing if it might be the bottle of perfume I hinted would make a good gift for dear ole mom.

But when I opened the gift on Christmas Eve, it wasn't what I thought at all. It wasn't even something I'd told him I wanted. It was something he wanted to give me. A kitchen appliance.

A more expensive gift. And something I needed.

So many years ago, the world also waited to receive the gift of a boy. Only this gift could never be bought. This gift of a boy wrapped in swaddling clothes was actually God wrapped in human flesh who came to save us.

A gift more expensive than we imagined and not exactly what we expected. Something we needed.

God came. Camouflaged in human flesh. Fully God and fully man. The gift giver is also the gift.

We can become so busy amid the hustle and bustle of the Christmas season, we might forget the wonder of it all. How incredible it is that

God would give us such a gift. He made a way for us to be in a right relationship with Him again through His beloved Son.

Through Him we receive many wonderful things:

- Forgiveness of sins
- Grace and mercy
- Eternal life in heaven

This Christmas, seek Him like the wise men and shepherds did so long ago and find Him.

There's a gift with your name on it wrapped in camouflage—waiting for you to discover what's really inside. Jesus—the gift of a boy.

> *She will give birth to a son, and you are to give him the name Jesus, because he will save his people from their sins.* (Matthew 1:21)

Merry Christmas!

• CHAPTER 32 •

Lit

HAVE YOU EVER LOOKED back at something from childhood and wondered, *What in tarnation was I thinking?*

As children, we had a blast trying to catch enough fireflies to make a night light for our bedrooms using a canning jar.

Sometimes though, we used to hold the bug until its tail lit up nice and bright and then pinched it off. We rubbed its glowing bottom on our fingers and pretended we were wearing shiny, diamond rings.

What in the world?

We flashed our fingers around in the dark, lit up with glowing bug butts, and pretended we were rich. We didn't give one iota about the poor bug missing part of its body. (I'm embarrassed to say I even I did this.)

I know it's just a bug. But I can't help but think I killed a lot of God's unique critters for my own personal temporary glory. I loved seeing my fingers aglow, shining in the dark summer night.

Now, I'd never pinch the tail from a lightning bug and put it on my finger. Instead, I'm in awe of God's handiwork and creativity. *How did He make a bug that glows?*

Since I've grown up, I find I still like shiny things. But as a Christian, I desire to represent God well here on earth. How do I shine my light in a way that doesn't involve lightning bugs and personal glory?

> *"You are the light of the world. A town built on a hill cannot be hidden. Neither do people light a lamp and put it under a bowl. Instead they put it on its stand, and it gives light to everyone in the house. In the same way, let your light shine before others, that they may see your good deeds and glorify your Father in heaven." (Matthew 5:14–17)*

When I read that casually, I think, *Oh, I know. I'll be the light by doing good deeds and then others will see my light shining.* But that's backwards.

In the passage, Jesus said let your light shine before others. **Then** he said that they may see your good deeds. Subconsciously, I wanted to insert some personal glory. I wanted my good deeds to be the light. He also said, "You are the light."

So, how do we become the light?

When we are born again and filled with the Holy Spirit, we are **"lit."**

We become the "light of the world" at that moment. We don't do good works to light up the world. The good deeds are a result of us being reborn through the power of the Holy Spirit.

What Are the Effects of Being Lit?

- We are the light.
- We're on fire for God.
- We fall madly in love with Jesus.
- We shine through the power of the Holy Spirit.
- We do good deeds.

Like moths are drawn to a flame, others are drawn to our light and then **see** our good works. This brings God glory.

So, shine on, my friend. No lightning bugs needed.

Prayer

> *Heavenly Father, fill us with Your powerful Holy Spirit so we are born again. Make us the light of the world so others are drawn to You. In the mighty name of Jesus Christ, Amen.*

· CHAPTER 33 ·

Seeds

IN FIRST GRADE, I made a plant.

Everyone in class did. We placed potting soil into Styrofoam cups and tucked tiny seeds beneath the soil. Then we lined the cups up on the counter in the sunlight and, each day, gave the seed a bit of water.

What I recall most is the day the tender shoots popped up through the soil. I'd made a plant.

I carried it home on the school bus when it grew bigger and showed my parents what I'd done.

As I held the sweet, little plant in my hands, a bubble of pride bloomed inside my young heart.

But all I did to make the plant grow was give it what it needed—soil, sun, and water. The seed already contained everything necessary to bloom into a beautiful plant before I ever placed it in the dirt. I followed the teacher's instructions. I watered it and made sure it had sunlight.

Then I waited.

It did the miraculous thing God created it to do and became what He designed. A beautiful little plant. That part was completely out of my control.

As Christians, we plant spiritual seeds. It comes naturally because we want to share with others what God has done in our lives. We encourage family, friends, and coworkers to trust Him in every area of their lives because He alone is trustworthy.

In childhood, I followed the directions of my teacher and gave the seed soil, sunlight, and water so it could grow into a plant. Spiritually, we follow our teacher's directions and give others what they need. We point them to Jesus.

Sometimes, we never see tender spiritual shoots pop up through the soil from the seed we planted. But sometimes, we do.

That's when we might do the same thing I did as a child. We might feel a little bubble of pride thinking we've done some great thing for God. When, really, God has done the great thing. We planted a seed in the garden of someone's heart soil already prepared by God to receive it.

> *For we are God's handiwork, created in Christ Jesus to do*
> *good works, which God prepared in advance for us to do.*
> *(Ephesians 2:10)*

Personally, I can't keep my mouth shut about God. I might get on some people's nerves. But I won't close my mouth. I won't stop writing about the wonderful things He does. I can't. I'd burst if I didn't let it out.

So, while you're planting seeds this spring remember those spiritual seeds and point others to Jesus. Just don't put pressure on yourself about whether or not it sprouts into a plant. That's God's job.

Prayer

> *Heavenly Father, thank You for working in our lives in such a powerful way that we can't keep our mouths shut about it. Give us the words to share with others who need to hear them. Give us the words to write to touch the hearts of those who need to read them. In the powerful name of Jesus, Amen.*

• CHAPTER 34 •

Six Feet Apart

Record my misery; list my tears on your scroll—are they not in your record? (Psalm 56:8)

THOSE WERE CRAZY SOCIAL distancing times we were living in during 2020. The stores had signs on the floor, outside on the sidewalk, and there seemed to be reminders all over the place that we needed to stay at least six feet apart. I couldn't see one of the signs about social distancing without being reminded of a woman I saw lying on the ground in a local cemetery. She, too, must stay six feet apart from someone but it's way harder than social distancing.

I DROVE BY THE cemetery every day on my way home from work. One day, I glanced over and saw a woman lying on the ground. I did a double take—*yes*. She was wearing shorts, lying flat on her back, beside a grave, staring up at the sky.

What in the world?

Maybe she's trying out a spot? You know, lying on the ground, wondering what it would be like to lay there for eternity. Or maybe she's in *deep* grief.

I thought of her all evening and mentioned the strange event to my husband.

Then, a couple of days later, again I saw her in the graveyard. Sitting in the same spot, patting the grass near her. My heart ached and I felt an urge to go talk to her.

No. Too personal. She'll think I'm crazy. Yet, again, I thought of her throughout the evening. *Who has died she loved so much? A spouse? A parent? A child?*

A few days later, I saw her again. I slowed down and almost pulled in but kept driving as my mind raced. I thought of turning around several times but, instead, dialed my sister when I pulled into my driveway. It's been four years since she lost her son, Brandon.

"You should talk to her," she advised when I explained my plight of wanting to stop but not wanting to intrude on her personal grief. "I always wanted to talk about Brandon. She won't think you're crazy."

I swallowed. "Okay, I'm going back." I turned around in my driveway and headed back to the cemetery. I prayed for God to give me words. *How do I even approach this woman? Maybe she'll be gone by the time I get there and I can avoid this altogether but still get brownie points with God for making an effort.*

I pulled into the cemetery and drove around the big circle. She was sitting inside her vehicle by this time staring at her cell phone with her window cracked. I pulled up beside her and rolled down the passenger side window not sure what she'd think about my stopping with social distancing and all.

"I've noticed you in the graveyard a lot lately."

She nodded and stepped out of her vehicle. I discovered she'd lost her oldest son, Austin. He'd passed away from a pulmonary embolism. He was twenty-one years old and it was the eighth-month anniversary of his death. As we talked, she shared a couple of photos of him.

She had a blister on her hand from trimming the grass on his grave with a pair of scissors.

She told me the story of how he died. I'm sure she's told it a hundred times but to me it was new and fresh and *awful*. She *misses him* terribly.

God knows what we're going through. He knows about every spilled tear and when we're consumed with waves of deep grief. He knows our every thought and inclination. He knows when we need someone to stop and talk to us. He will bring others into our path to remind us He knows and cares about what we're going through.

While some are trying to stay at least six feet apart because of a virus, He knows some are staying six feet apart because of death. The separation isn't forever.

One day, a precious grieving mother will hold her beloved son in her arms once more. Never to be six feet apart again.

Until then, he's always in her heart.

In honor of a devoted, loving mother and a precious son gone too soon.

Crystal and Austin

• CHAPTER 35 •

The Pressure Cooker

Five Ways to Let Off Steam without Blowing Your Top

I HATED THE PRESSURE cooker when I was growing up. It hissed and made strange noises. I expected it to blow up every time Mom used it. My bedroom was beside the kitchen, so I had to walk by the scary thing every time I left my room. I'd dash by the stove as fast as I could in case it blew its top.

If you're unfamiliar, the *pressure cooker* is a sealed, stainless-steel pot used to cook food under *high* pressure. It expels steam from the contraption on the lid and makes scary, hissing sounds.

Nowadays, they make a similar digital cooker and it doesn't scare the living daylights out of small children. Thank goodness.

I can relate to the cooker as an adult. Sometimes, I feel under pressure and need to vent and let off steam. I'm sure many others feel this way when dealing with the stresses of life.

In general, I'm pretty easy going. But sometimes, I'll get hot over something and stew in anger. Then, like the dreaded cooker, I'm about to blow my top. It takes *a lot* for me to get to that point. But when I do, watch out.

Fools give full vent to their rage, but the wise bring calm in the end. (Proverbs 29:11)

God warns against doing what comes *naturally* to us. We want to relieve the strain and give full vent to our rage. I've made that mistake and it only does more harm. It might make us feel better to blow up at someone but more than likely, we'll regret our reaction later.

Here are five ways to let off steam without blowing your top.

1. Walk it off! Go for a long walk or run. Exercise helps and gives time for thought before making a calm response.

2. Rearrange furniture. This is a good way to release those pinned up frustrations and burn off that negative energy.

3. Write. It helps to write down what's making us angry and why. Sometimes, this simple action can alleviate the anger.

4. Read. Reading takes our minds off the problem for a little while. Giving us time to calm down.

5. Cook. Make comfort food and go ahead and eat some. Calories don't count. They're called "comfort foods" for a reason. While enjoying the delicious food, think of ways to handle the situation without causing harm.

When the scary cooker has done its job, the meat is tender and delicious. The high pressure worked. The same is true with us. We grow up a little when we stop allowing anger to explode out of us and take time to calm down. Our reactions reveal character and growth. Even though it's hard to remain cool when we feel steamed, God allows these situations for our benefit.

He's working all things for our good and is at *work* making us better and *more* like Jesus.

> *And we know that in all things God works for the good of those who love him, who have been called according to his purpose. (Romans 8:28)*

• CHAPTER 36 •

If the Good Lord's Willing . . . .

RECENTLY, WHEN I WAS home, I took Mom to dialysis early on a Saturday morning and the creek was up. It wasn't high enough to worry about crossing but reminded me of her wise words from childhood.

"If the good Lord's willing and the creek don't rise."

They echoed in my mind all day. Mom used that phrase countless times in my life. So, as I left, on my way out of her driveway, I snapped some pictures of the risen water. I pondered the common phrase about God's will and the creek.

Because sometimes, what we want is *not* God's will. And sometimes the creek does rise.

It can rise to the point that we are unable to get across and it's dangerous if we try.

It can prevent us from getting where we want to go in life. Then we have to turn around and go in a direction we didn't plan on. It can be discouraging. It can even hurt. We may have to swallow our pride when our plans don't work out.

God warns us about our plans and His will.

> *Now listen, you who say, "Today or tomorrow we will go to this or that city, spend a year there, carry on business and make money." Why, you do not even know what will happen tomorrow. What is your life? You are a mist that appears for a little while and then vanishes. Instead, you ought to say, "If it is the Lord's will, we will live and do this or that." As it is, you boast in your arrogant schemes. All such boasting is evil. If anyone, then, knows the good they ought to do and doesn't do it, it is sin for them. (James 4:13–17)*

"God is large and in charge," Mom said when I recently broke down in tears during a phone call. I had to accept something terrible that I hated. It wasn't fair and my heart was broken. I didn't get what I planned on and wanted. I hated seeing those I love completely crushed as their hearts broke, too.

We had to accept what happened as God's will. There was no way to stop it and there was no way to go back and change it.

Mom is right about the creek and she's right about God. But it's difficult when God's not willing and the creek does rise.

It's hard....

- when we lose someone we dearly love.
- when we see someone suffering from an illness.
- when we don't get what we desperately want.

The list could go on and on. But under God's sovereign authority is the best place for us to be. He knows the plans He has for us. (Jeremiah 29:11) His plans are for *our good and not to harm us.*

How can we honor God when the creek rises?

Seek God's will in our lives even when it's hard.

These days, going home is sometimes hard. There's a small family graveyard along my parent's road that's slowly growing larger.

My oldest sister, Kathy, is buried there. My beloved nephew, Brandon, is buried there. Now, my precious Daddy is there, too. It makes me sad to drive by the cemetery.

Our lives are truly a mist. The older I get the faster life passes by. None of us knows when our time is up. It's best to roll with the punches and hit our knees often. Seeking God in all things because He has our best interest at heart *always.*

• CHAPTER 37 •

He Will Carry Me

WE JUST GOT BACK from a wonderful beach vacation

We haven't taken a family vacation for about five years, it seems. So, we thoroughly enjoyed ourselves. The downside was that we got there when a hurricane was hitting the gulf. But it was a Category One and we weren't directly in it's path. When we arrived, the water was all the way up to the dunes and as muddy as the Mississippi River.

Even though the conditions were not ideal for relaxation, we figured we'd never be at the beach again *during* a hurricane, so we tried to make the best of a bad situation. It was definitely exciting.

So, we went shopping and drove to see sights the next day because the beach was too wild to enjoy. Wind and waves, wind and waves. But by the next day, we could go sit on the beach and listen to that wonderful relaxing sound of waves rolling in and splashing on the sand.

By the last full day we had to enjoy the beach, it was finally the way I imagined our vacation would be. The brown water cleared up as the shoreline receded from the dunes and there were more folks enjoying the day alongside us on the beach.

There was a little girl there about seven or eight years old who spent the majority of the day using a skimboard directly in front of us. She had some pretty good skills, I must say!

As we were about to leave the beach and go eat dinner, I noticed that she and her daddy were walking out into the ocean together. Each time a big wave came, they'd jump and walk on farther out. Eventually, he was holding her hand and then finally she was riding on his back with her arms wrapped around his neck. (How I wish I would have snapped a picture of this!)

I was reminded of a dream I had right before we went on vacation where my dad was with me and I was hugging his back in a similar way and he said, "What a wonderful surprise!" Then he called me by my nickname he rarely uses *these* days. When I awoke from the dream, I pondered it and realized it's been a long time since he called me that and I haven't hugged his back since childhood.

Seeing the little girl in the ocean with her dad brought back to memory the *safety* I felt riding on my daddy's back when I was young. I completely trusted that he would carry me safely to our destination, wherever that might be.

I took a break from my daily Bible reading while we were traveling so when we got home, I settled back into my routine. I was taken aback by some of the first verses I read considering the little girl riding on her daddy's back was still fresh in my mind.

> *"Listen to me, you descendants of Jacob, all the remnant of the people of Israel, you whom I have upheld since your birth, and have carried since you were born. Even to your old age and gray hairs I am he, I am he who will sustain you. I have made you and I will carry you; I will sustain you and I will rescue you. (Isaiah 46:3–4)*

Honestly, I read it over and over. I found great comfort in those words.

I know that God demonstrated this to me before we left for vacation with the dream and while we were at the beach with a picture of a little girl clinging to her daddy's back with her arms wrapped tightly around his neck as he walked her out into the great depths of the ocean. The water was over her head, but it was **not** over his.

No matter what the future holds, and even when I'm old and gray, I know **He will carry me.**

PS, I'm not that far away from old and gray . . . tee hee ✕

• CHAPTER 37 •

The Heart of It

MY PARENTS ALWAYS *SLICED* a watermelon when I was young.

We kids would grab a slice, sit on the porch together, and a seed-spitting competition would begin! Definitely a happy childhood memory!

At some point, when I became an adult and paid for my own watermelons, I decided that scooping it out into a dish was my preferred way to eat it. Slices are too *messy*.

Once, when we were staying with my in-laws, I bought a watermelon and helped myself to some in my usual way. Later on that evening, my father-in-law took the foil off the partially eaten watermelon sitting in the fridge and with great shock at what he uncovered said, "Who took the heart right out of the watermelon?!"

I said, "Umm . . . me." Suddenly realizing that he was old-school and thought scooping the heart out of it was the WRONG way to eat a watermelon!

He might be right.

The heart is the *best* part and when it's gone, the rest of the watermelon is not quite the same. It's still good but it gets more distasteful the farther you get from the heart and the closer you get to the bitter rind. Then what's left gets thrown out.

Sometimes, we do this same thing in life. We take the best part and leave the rest. I guess it's human nature.

As a woman, I know that this happens to us. We give and give of ourselves until we have nothing left taking care of our homes, families, spouses, and working jobs. Then we walk around feeling empty because the *heart* is gone and that's a tough place to be. Empty, numb, and sometimes bitter.

When we get so far from the heart of things, we just want to get the sweetness of life back.

We want to get back to the **heart** of it all. I'm so glad that God *gives* the best part instead of taking it.

When we have nothing left and it seems that all the good parts have been scooped out, is when He fills us up again . . . to *overflowing*.

He *never* fails. **Trust Him.**

> *Create in me a pure heart, O God, and renew a steadfast spirit within me. (Psalm 51:10)*

• CHAPTER 38 •

Super Salad!

ONE NIGHT MY HUSBAND took me on a date to one of our favorite places. I love the restaurant because of the soup they serve as an appetizer. It's chicken and rice which is *delicious*. There was no doubt that I wanted the soup to start the meal. :)

My husband and I discussed what we would order while the waitress was getting our drinks. By the time she came back, we both knew we wanted steaks. When she asked what I'd like, I happily answered her, "We both want the same thing! The Club Steak. I'd also like soup and a salad."

"Oh, you get a super salad." She said, "What *other* side would you like?"

"I get another side? Hmm . . . Let me see." I looked at the list of sides on the menu and chose spinach because I'm trying to cut my carbohydrates. Even though I'm not a huge fan of spinach.

She left with our orders and I turned to my husband and said, "Well, guess we get extra sides. I'm getting soup, a super salad, and spinach with my steak."

He looked at me cockeyed and said, "*Super salad?*"

"Uh huh . . . she said I got a super salad."

He laughed and said, "She said soup **or** salad . . . not a *super salad!*"

"*What?!* I thought I was getting a super salad."

The disappointment must have been all over my face because my husband said, "I can tell her not to bring the spinach and you can just get a salad in place of it."

"No!" I responded quickly, "I'll just eat the spinach. I do not want to tell her I thought she offered me a 'super salad.'"

We received the yummy soup shortly thereafter and enjoyed it along with a laugh over the "super salad" incident.

What can I say? I *literally* thought she offered me a **super salad.**

In my defense, I told her that I wanted club steak, soup, and salad. So . . . I can't take ALL the blame for the miscommunication . . . .

I heard her incorrectly or at least that's what I thought she said.

But I was WRONG.

How often do we do this same thing with God? He says one thing and we hear what we want to hear or we do not hear Him correctly.

> *Come, my children, listen to me; I will teach you the fear of the LORD. (Psalm 34:11)*

• CHAPTER 39 •

If They Die

IN MARCH 2011, MY nephew, Brandon Bourbon came to visit me in Tennessee with his girlfriend, Nicole. I was so *excited* because I don't get visitors from home often and he wanted to go to *church* with me. I'll never forget proudly introducing him to fellow church members at Temple Baptist Church in White House, Tennessee where we were members at the time. I introduced him to the Pastor, the Youth Pastor and anybody else who noticed my tall, good-looking, football playing nephew!

I don't remember the sermon that day but I'll never forget how happy I was to have him with me in the service.

After church, we took Brandon and Nicole to eat at our favorite Chinese buffet. Then we went home, played soccer in the back yard (where I realized I'm getting too old to play soccer with college kids!) and hung out until evening.

I'm glad I snapped a picture of him (and Nicole) in our front yard that day. After which, he climbed up the tree next to us, giving everyone a good laugh!

When I was very young, a friend once asked me, "How do you know if you love somebody?" I remember thinking about it a second and then I replied, "If they die and you cry...then you loved them." She thought that made pretty good sense and I've never forgotten that conversation from my childhood. I guess because it is true.

Since I was a kid, I've lost some relatives along the way but nothing hit me as hard as hearing my sister tell me that my nephew, Brandon, had taken his own life. We were all in shock. Brandon was not depressed that any of us were aware of. What is this about? We had tons of questions and nothing made sense.

We went home for the funeral and I must say how proud I was of our little town of Potosi, Missouri. Brandon was a bit of a hometown hero because of his football successes, and they wanted to turn on the football field lights for him - one more time.

The funeral was on the high school football field and it was packed. There were three buses of football players from Kansas University and Washburn University where he played college football. First, his high school teammates went through the line and left jerseys on the casket.

Then Kansas University football players went through then Washburn University. I've *never seen* so many big guys with tears streaking down their cheeks.

It was evident that those who spoke, truly loved Brandon. The most touching part of the funeral was at the end when the Superintendent of schools said, "Something isn't right about this whole thing. Brandon was never on the 50 yard line. He was always at the in-zone."

Then Brandon's blockers came up and carried his casket to the in-zone one last time for one final touchdown. There was silence until he reached the in-zone and then cheers erupted in the crowd along with complete breakdowns of tears by some. The whole service completely honored his life.

Brandon was just a really great kid who made everyone proud of him. He was in love with God. His life reflects that and God was all he could talk about according to his best friend, Dylan who spoke at his funeral. I can only imagine the impact he would have had if he would have become a youth pastor or ministered to youth in some way because kids loved Brandon!

He was the type to play outside with the little kids throwing a football when everyone else was inside talking. My son, Joseph, came out of his room shortly after Brandon's death carrying a football with a KU logo on it and showed it to me. He said that he and Brandon were playing catch outside one day and Brandon gave it to him. Now, it is a treasure to Joseph.

There is NO question that Brandon was *deeply loved* and is already dearly missed. He was beloved to those of us lucky enough to know him.

My childhood logic about love stands true, "If they die and you cry... then you *loved* them."

I've *never* seen so many tears.

Love one another deeply, from the heart. 1st Peter 1:22

Janet and Brandon

• CHAPTER 40 •

A Gift to Remember

IT WAS CHRISTMAS EVE.

Mr. and Mrs. Nichols expected their family to arrive soon for dinner. The fragrant aroma of stuffed turkey wafted through the small farmhouse. Mrs. Nichols hummed "Jingle Bells" as she cooked.

"It's snowing," Mr. Nichols announced as he peered out the living room window overlooking their land. No other houses were in sight just an old barn, rolling hills, and fields.

"Oh dear. I hope everyone arrives safely," Mrs. Nichols said as she wiped her wet hands on her apron.

Mr. Nichols turned to his wife and asked, "Who?"

"Our children, Kate and Annie." She held back her irritation and exhaled. "You remember, *your* daughters," she said.

He shook his head with a blank stare.

"Well, they'll be here soon, along with the grandchildren."

"I ain't old enough to have grandchildren." He chuckled.

She mumbled under her breath and added a pat of butter to the mashed potatoes warming on the stove top.

A few minutes later, in came their two daughters with their husbands. They carried wrapped packages and covered dishes of aromatic foods. Four children bustled through the door behind them.

"Merry Christmas, Dad." Kate hugged her father after setting down her gifts.

"Christmas?" He scratched his head, confused. "I sure didn't know it was Christmas."

When Annie finished placing her dishes on the counter for the meal, she tightly hugged him, too, and said, "Merry Christmas, Daddy."

"Well . . . Merry Christmas, I reckon," he said. Then he made himself comfortable and sat down in the recliner near the window as the little house brimmed with vaguely familiar people.

The daughters helped their mother prepare the meal in the kitchen as the grandchildren made themselves at home.

"Pops, where's your tree?" The youngest grandchild, Claire, held a small wrapped gift in her hand.

"My tree?" The old man motioned out the window. "Why, it's out there with all the other trees."

"Not *those* trees," Claire said with a giggle, "your Christmas tree."

"Christmas tree?"

"Yeah. We have a great big one in our living room. It's got lots of decorations and we put our presents under it." She held up the gift in her hand. "I got this for you and I want to put it under your tree."

Kate answered for her father from the kitchen, "Pops and Grandma don't have a Christmas tree, honey. They haven't had one in many years. Not since I was little, like you." Then she added, "Not everyone has a Christmas tree."

Claire's mouth dropped open. "They don't?"

"Dinner is ready," Mrs. Nichols interrupted. She guided Claire to the small folding table set up in the kitchen for her grandchildren. After the blessing, they gobbled up turkey and dressing.

Pops finished eating before everyone else. He rose from the table and began rifling through the kitchen cabinets. Then he took the lids off every container he found on the counters until Mrs. Nichols asked, "What on earth are you looking for?"

"Where's the divinity?" He grumbled as he looked in the cabinet under the kitchen sink, "We can't have Christmas without divinity." It was his favorite candy.

"I've got some. I made it for you yesterday." She scurried to her bedroom and returned with a round tin. She popped the top off revealing white pieces of fluffy candy. "Here you go, dear," she said as she handed it to him.

He smiled with great satisfaction as if he'd found some wonderful thing he'd lost many years earlier. He happily munched on the candy. It became oddly quiet when he asked Mrs. Nichols, "Mom, when I get married someday, will you teach my wife to make this for me? You make the best divinity."

"I will," she answered and without missing a beat, added, "I'm sure you'll marry a beautiful, young woman who's a *great* cook."

Everyone smiled knowingly. These types of conversations were becoming common as he worsened with Alzheimer's. Though some of his actions were jarring, like trying to use the television remote control as a telephone, they tried to make the best of a bad situation as he declined.

They finished the meal and began clearing the table.

Mr. Nichols relaxed, gazing out the window at the falling snow. He popped another piece of fluffy candy into his mouth, savoring its sweetness.

The grandchildren sat around the coffee table playing games except for Claire. She plopped down on the floor next to her grandfather who was kicked back in the recliner.

"Why don't you have a Christmas tree, Pops?"

"Who says I don't?"

"Mom did."

"Oh . . . well . . . ." he began to explain but couldn't finish his thought, "I can't remember exactly." Then he held the tin of candy out and offered some to the little girl, "Try some. Mom makes the best candy."

Claire picked out a piece with no nuts and took a bite. She smiled as it melted inside her mouth. "Yummy."

"Told ya." Pops smiled as a glint of familiarity shone in his eyes. Claire reminded him of himself at that age. Before he got tired of the world turning Christmas into one big sale. Before he'd banned trees from the house and all the other decorations that accompanied the special holiday. Before he *couldn't* remember.

"You wanna open the present I brought you?" Claire asked.

"Sure do." His eyes lit with excitement as the little girl handed it to him. The rowdy game of Yahtzee going on at the kitchen table continued and nobody noticed the giving of the gift.

He gently pulled the red ribbon from the package. Then he tore the paper off and discovered a handmade ornament inside. A small cross made of beads.

"I made it in Sunday school. It's a cross and see this . . . ." Claire held out the looped fishing line tied to the top of it, "That's what you use to hang it on the tree." The little girl explained, "It's to remember Jesus dying on the cross for us."

Pops held up the ornament by the clear line as it twirled around. His eyes filled with tears as he remembered Christmas when he was a boy. He *remembered* his deep love for Jesus. He cleared his throat and said, "I'll never forget that." He hugged his granddaughter and whispered in a cracked voice, "Thank you."

"You're welcome," Claire said with a smile that quickly turned to a frown, "but you don't have a tree to hang it on."

"Come with me," he said and placed the ornament in the pocket of his flannel shirt. He stepped into his leather boots that were beside his chair and the two of them made their way to the kitchen door that led to the garage.

Mrs. Nichols, always keeping an eye on her husband of fifty years, asked, "Where are you two going?"

"I got something to show this little whippersnapper in the garage."

"Alright, but please don't go outside," she advised.

"We won't." He winked at the child as they closed the door behind them. Once they were in the garage, he turned to her and said, "You wait here and I'll be right back." He opened the side door in the garage and headed out into the snowy, dark night as the child waited.

It didn't take him long to return. He stepped back inside the garage holding a little cedar tree with muddy roots dangling from it. He shook off the remaining snow from its branches then closed the garage door behind him.

Claire's eyes lit up, "Is that your Christmas tree?"

Mr. Nichols nodded. "I used to have one just like this. Now, we need a bucket to put it in and some rocks or something," he rubbed his chin whiskers and gazed around the cluttered garage as he said, "then we can decorate it."

"Yeah, but where are the decorations?"

"Only got this one," he pulled the beaded cross from his pocket as he evaluated the contents of the garage. There were empty gas cans, used flower pots, and a bag of cement. Then he found an empty five-gallon bucket. "This'll work," he said as he grabbed it by the handle.

"Look!" Claire pointed to a partially used bag of potting soil tucked away in the corner. They used it to fill up the bucket. Then they planted the little cedar tree. It was as pretty as any Christmas tree could be.

"Put the ornament on it, Pops!" Claire said with dimples forming in both cheeks as she grinned.

Mr. Nichols hung the beaded cross on the tree. With excitement glinting in his eyes, he said, "Let's show it to Mom."

They proudly took the tree inside the house and placed it on the kitchen table in the middle of the Yahtzee game.

"What on earth?!" Mrs. Nichols' eyes opened as wide as the lids would allow.

"Merry Christmas, Mom," Pops said with a sweet tone.

She sighed as a great smile spread across her tired face. The Alzheimer's that wore her down daily and brought frustration and tears had brought her a gift this day. It was the first Christmas tree they'd seen inside the house in over thirty years. And even though at the moment, her husband thought she was his own mother, she didn't seem to care.

"Merry Christmas, dear."

****This is a work of fiction to honor my beloved parents—Travis and Rachel Eye. Always loving us the **best** way they knew how.*

Shortly after my father's passing from Alzheimer's in 2019, Mom had a Christmas tree for the first time in many, many years. She passed away in November, 2022, leaving us with a giant hole in our hearts. So thankful for both of them.

CROSS MY HEART

Children, obey your parents in the Lord, for this is right. "Honor your father and mother"—which is the first commandment with a promise—"so that it may go well with you and that you may enjoy long life on the earth." (Ephesians 6:1–3)

***This short story was originally published 12/15/2019 in Rooted and Grounded—Spreading Good News, *a small newspaper in Kentucky.*

www.ingramcontent.com/pod-product-compliance
Lightning Source LLC
Chambersburg PA
CBHW071656090426
42738CB00009B/1548